The Risen Lord

Messages and Thoughts
on the
Resurrection of Jesus Christ

Jim Fowler

C.I.Y. Publishibg
17102 Blanco Trail
San Antonio, TX 78248

THE RISEN LORD

Messages and Thoughts on the Resurrection of Jesus Christ

Published by
C.I.Y. Publishing
17102 Blanco Trail
San Antonio, Texas 78248

ISBN 13 digit – 978-1-929541-37-9

Printed in the United States of America

FOREWORD

Looking back over thirty-five years of pastoral ministry and an additional ten years of conference ministry since retirement from pastoral ministry, Jim determined to select and compile ten messages on the extremely important subject of the resurrection of Jesus Christ.

During his thirty-five years of pastoral ministry Jim Fowler had numerous opportunities to preach on the risen Lord Jesus Christ. In this volume Jim has selected ten of his messages and thoughts on the resurrection of Jesus Christ and its meaning to Christian believers.

Jim's extensive theological training is evident in his thoughts and teaching. Many of his messages are more like theological treatises, rather than the "bottom-shelf" simplicity of many contemporary sermons in the churches of today.

At the same time, Jim repetitively emphasizes that the resurrection of Jesus Christ must be viewed beyond just historical and theological categories, allowing the experiential resurrection-life of the living Lord Jesus to be evidenced as the reality of Christian lives today.

Jim does not claim to have any new or novel information on the subject of the resurrection of Christ. He is a traditionalist in the sense that he seeks to nestle into the historic and orthodox dogma of the Church. He does believe, however, that the historic Christian teaching concerning the resurrection of our Lord has deteriorated into substantialist categories of historical and theological explication that has often diluted the explanation of the vital dynamic of Christ's resurrection-life as by the living Spirit of Christ.

These messages have not been reformatted into a more formal and technical style for their printed form. They retain the elements of verbal sermonic presentation.

The reader will note the repetition of ideas, scripture citations, and illustrative materials in these ten messages. Over a span of thirty-five years, it is inevitable that any preacher will utilize some of the same material, though hopefully in fresh and novel ways. Repetition and redundancy can serve a positive instructional purpose, as the repetition of affirmations provides a multilevel foundation of convincing belief. I take comfort in the fact that in the midst of God's creation there is abundant repetition, recurrence, and duplication whereby God sought to reveal Himself.

Jim Fowler
2022

CONTENTS

TELL ME WHY!

Many, if not most, Christians are unable to explain why the resurrection of Jesus is so important to the Christian gospel. Many would find themselves handicapped to even explain why Easter is the climax of the Christian year. There seems to be a pathetic ignorance among Christians concerning the meaning of the most important event in Jesus' life, and the implications of that event for all Christian people.

Christian teaching concerning the resurrection of Jesus Christ is often so defensive. Teachers and preachers (especially at the Easter season) often seek to defend the veracity of the historical reality of Christ's resurrection from the dead. Challenged by the skeptics to document the historicity of Jesus' life, death and resurrection, Christians apologetically defend His earthly existence and the recorded events of His life. They are especially delighted with the extra-biblical statement (as if the Biblical statements have less validity) of the Jewish historian, Josephus, who wrote near the end of the first century,

> "Now there was about this time Jesus, a wise man, if it be lawful to call him a man; for he was a doer of wonderful works, a teacher of such men as receive the truth with pleasure. He drew over to him many Jews, and also many of the Greeks. This man was the Christ. And when Pilate had condemned him to the cross, upon his impeachment by the principal man among us, those who had loved from

> the first did not forsake him, for *he appeared to them alive on the third day*, the divine prophets having spoken these and thousands of other wonderful things about him. And even now, the race of Christians, so named from him, has not died out."[1]

In addition to defending the historicity of Jesus, Christian teachers use the resurrection to defend the deity of Jesus. Challenged by those who question how Jesus could be the God-man who claimed to be "one with the Father" (cf. Jn. 10:30), Christians point to the historical resurrection of Jesus from the dead as the ultimate divine miracle that allegedly proves the deity of Jesus Christ as God. The historical resurrection of Jesus is employed as a logical leverage to authenticate and accredit important Christological formulation of the united deity and humanity of the person of Jesus.

The third emphasis of contemporary Christian teaching on the resurrection is to provide a defense of the Christian expectation of the eventual resurrection of Christians' bodies in the future. In the great "resurrection chapter" of I Corinthians 15, the apostle Paul certainly ties the historical resurrection of Jesus to the assurance of the bodily resurrection of Christians after death, but the predominance of Pauline references to the resurrection of Jesus are not linked to future expectation. A theology of future expectation alone may provide an incentive of hope, but often leaves people empty of the spiritual dynamic for living in the present.

When emphasis on the resurrection in Christian teaching is limited to the defense of the accuracy of Jesus' historicity, the authentication of His deity, and the assurance of the future bodily resurrection of believers, such apologetic-oriented Christian teaching is woefully deficient. Christian theology must go beyond this defensive orientation and articulation of explaining the import of the resurrection of Jesus, and proceed to a positive, affirmative theology of the resurrection and its impact for Christian lives.

People want to know ***why*** the historical resurrection of Jesus almost two millennia ago is of importance to the lives that they live now. The words of the popular campfire song, "*Tell me why*," keep coming to my mind:

Tell me why the stars do shine
Tell me why the ivy does twine
Tell me why the ocean's blue
And I will tell you just why I love you.

Because God made the stars to shine
Because God made the ivy to twine
Because God made the ocean's blue,
Because God made you, that's why I love you.

That is a nice little song, into which we could even read some romantic overtones. But, transferring the question of that song to the resurrection of Jesus, I have rewritten the words of the song to pose the question of the importance of Christ's resurrection:

Tell me why Christ rose from the grave.
Tell me why the ris'n Christ does save.
Tell me why Easter's victory,
And I will tell you why Christ lives in me.

I'll tell you why Christ rose from the grave.
I'll tell you why the ris'n Christ does save.
I'll tell you why Easter's victory,
Because Christ rose, and Christ lives in me.

What do these rewritten words indicate? We must proceed to consider the positive meaning and objective of the historical resurrection of Jesus Christ for Christians today. Christians must see and appreciate how the resurrection of Jesus extends to believers in every age.

In preparation for such discussion, let us ask three basic questions concerning what are arguably the three primary events of Jesus' life. In reference to the incarnation, the crucifixion, and the resurrection of Jesus, we are going to ask these questions: *What* happened? *Where* did it happen? and *Why* did it happen?

INCARNATION

What happened? A birth - A baby boy was born to Mary and Joseph (though Joseph was not the father). The child was conceived in the womb of Mary by the Holy Spirit.

Where did it happen? In Bethlehem in a manger-stall, when the Hebrew families were called to their familial towns to register for a census.

Why did it happen? The "Word became flesh" (Jn. 1:14) in the likeness of man (Phil. 2:6-8), the God-man. It was necessary that the Son of God should identify with humanity as the God-man. Why? Only a man could be tempted; only a man could die.

CRUCIFIXION

What happened? A death – an execution at the hands of Roman authorities as instigated by Jewish authorities under false pretenses.

Where did it happen? On a Roman cross on the hill of Golgotha – Calvary – outside the walls of the city of Jerusalem.

Why did it happen? Jesus Christ voluntarily submitted to death in order to vicariously and substitutionally take the death consequences of sin upon Himself. But death could not hold him, for He was sinless (Acts 2:24).

The Roman Catholic portion of the Christian church has tended to emphasize the incarnation, the birth of Jesus, the importance of Mary, but not to the diminishment of the suffering, the "passion" of the crucifixion and the implications of Jesus' death. The Protestant portion of the Christian church has tended to emphasize the crucifixion, the cross, the dying, the death, extending such into such experiential implications of "dying to self."

When presenting the events of Jesus' life to the world, birth (incarnation) and death (crucifixion) are natural phenomena grasped more easily by natural man, while resurrection is a supernatural phenomenon more difficult to explain "what happened?" – more difficult to produce a symbol for. The tragic situation is that the church has often diluted and "watered down" the emphasis on the resurrection to make the gospel more palatable – emphasizing the manger and the cross, Bethlehem and Golgotha (Calvary), and de-emphasizing the resurrection. Many Easter sermons will emphasize Jesus' death on the cross rather than the resurrection. This is tragic! Above all else, it is the resurrection that defines the Christian faith! We have often presented a deficient theology of resurrection.

RESURRECTION

What happened? A restoration to life out of death. This reemergence of life from death is even called a rebirth.

Acts 13:33 – "He (God) raised up Jesus, as it is also written in the second Psalm, 'You are My Son; today I have begotten You.'"

Col. 1:18 – "He (Jesus) is the beginning, the firstborn from the dead."

Rev. 1:5 – "Jesus Christ, the faithful witness, the firstborn of the dead"

Rom. 8:29 – "those whom He foreknew, He also predestined to become conformed to the image of His Son, so that He would be the firstborn among many brethren"

Where did it happen? - In the borrowed tomb that was discovered to be empty.

Why did it happen? To facilitate and enact the restoration of God's life in man, and that by a restorative spiritual rebirth.

Rom. 4:25 – "He was delivered over because of our transgressions, and was raised because of our justification."

To this event we will had a fourth question: *How* is the "why" question enacted?

This is of extreme and ultimate importance, for this is what Christianity is all about. Christian truth is not just the recitation of historical events. Christian truth is not just the theological formulation of interpreting historical events. Christian truth is the vital dynamic of the life of the risen and living Lord Jesus living in receptive Christians today (and forever). If we do not understand how the historical event of Jesus' resurrection connects to the living reality of Jesus Christ in us by the indwelling presence of His Spirit, we do not understand the gospel.

How is the life of God restored to man by the resurrection of Jesus Christ?

Jesus explained that His presence by the Spirit would be available to His followers:

John 14:16,17 – "I will ask the Father, and He will give you another Helper, that He may be with you forever; *that is* the Spirit of truth, whom the world cannot receive, because it does not see Him or know Him, *but* you know Him because He abides with you and will be in you.

John 14:26 – "But the Helper, the Holy Spirit, whom the Father will send in My name, He will teach you all things, and bring to your remembrance all that I said to you."

John 15:26 – "When the Helper comes, whom I will send to you from the Father, *that is* the Spirit of truth who proceeds from the Father, He will testify about Me"

John 16:7 – "if I do not go away, the Helper will not come to you; but if I go, I will send Him to you."

John 16:13-14 – "But when He, the Spirit of truth, comes, He will guide you into all the truth; for He will not speak on His own initiative, but whatever He hears, He will speak; and He will disclose to you what is to come. He will glorify Me, for He will take of Mine and will disclose *it* to you."

The promise of the Spirit was explained again –

Acts 1:8 – "you will receive power when the Holy Spirit has come upon you; and you shall be My witnesses both in Jerusalem, and in all Judea and Samaria, and even to the remotest part of the earth."

The promised Spirit of Christ appeared on Pentecost –

Acts 2:1-4 – "When the day of Pentecost had come, they were all together in one place. And suddenly there came from heaven a noise like a violent rushing wind, and it filled the whole house where they were sitting. And there appeared to them tongues as of fire distributing themselves, and they rested on each one of them. And they were all filled with the Holy Spirit and began to speak with other tongues, as the Spirit was giving them utterance."

Peter explained what had happened:

Acts 2:29-36 – "he (David) looked ahead and spoke of the resurrection of the Christ, that He was neither abandoned to Hades, nor did His flesh suffer decay. This Jesus God raised up again, to which we are all witnesses. Therefore, having been exalted to the right hand of God, and having received from the Father the promise of the Holy Spirit, He has poured forth this which you both see and hear. For it was not David who ascended into heaven, but he himself says:

> 'The Lord said to my Lord, "Sit at My right hand, Until I make Your enemies a footstool for Your feet."'

Therefore, let all the house of Israel know for certain that God has made Him both Lord and Christ—this Jesus whom you crucified."

I Cor. 15:45 – "the last Adam became a *life*-giving Spirit."

II Cor. 3:6 – "the Spirit gives *life*"

II Cor. 3:17 – "The Lord is the Spirit, and where the Spirit of the Lord is, there is liberty."

Rom. 1:4 – "He was declared the Son of God with power by the resurrection from the dead, according to the Spirit of holiness, Jesus Christ our Lord."

Rom. 8:9 – "If any man does not have the Spirit of Christ, he is none of His."

Rom. 8:11 – "If the Spirit of Him who raised Jesus from the dead dwells in you, He who raised Christ Jesus from the dead will also give *life* to your mortal bodies through His Spirit who dwells in you."

John 11:25 – "I am the resurrection and the *life*"

John 14:6 – I am the way, the truth and the *life*; no one comes to the Father but through Me."

John 10:10 – "I came that you might have *life*, and have it more abundantly."

I John 5:11,12 – "God has given us eternal *life*, and this *life* is in His son. He who has the Son has the *life*; he who does not have the Son of God does not have the life."

Col. 3:4 – "Christ who is our *life*"

How do we appropriate that risen life of Jesus?

I Pet. 1:3 – "God...according to His great mercy has caused us to be born again to a living hope through the resurrection of Jesus Christ from the dead."

John 3:1-8 – "Truly, truly, I say unto you, that unless one is born from above he cannot see the kingdom of God. ... unless one is born of water and the Spirit he cannot enter the kingdom of God. ... You must be born from above."

John 5:24 – He who believes Him who sent Me, has eternal *life*, and does not come into judgment, but has passed out of death into *life*."

I John 3:14 – "We know that we have passed out of death into *life*, because we love the brethren."

Eph. 2:4,5 – "But God, being rich in mercy, because of His great love with which He loved us, even when we were dead in our transgressions, made us *alive* together with Christ."

Rom. 6:4,5 – "We have been buried with Him through baptism into death, so that as Christ was raised from the dead through the glory of the Father, so we too might walk in newness of *life*. For if we have become united with Him in the likeness of His death, certainly we shall also be in the likeness of His resurrection.

Rom. 6:11 – "Consider yourselves to be dead to sin, but *alive* to God in Christ Jesus."

Col. 2:12 – "we have been buried with Him in baptism, in which you were also raised up with Him through faith in the working of God, who raised Him from the dead. When you were dead in your transgressions and the uncircumcision of your flesh, He made you *alive* together with Him."

Col. 3:1 – "Therefore if you have been raised up with Christ, keep seeking the things above, where Christ is, seated at the right hand of God."

II Cor. 5:17 – If any man is in Christ, he is a *new creature*; old things have passed away, behold all things have become new."

Eph. 4:24; Col. 3:10 – You have put off the old man, you have put on the *new man*."

Paul's deepest desire: Phil. 3:10,11 – "That I might know Him and the power of His resurrection and the fellowship of His sufferings, being conformed to His death, in order that I may attain to the resurrection from the dead."

NOTE – the ultimate objective of Christian life is not to get to heaven, and avoid hell as a fire insurance policy – the great escape. God's desire is that we be fit for earth on the way to heaven – continuum.

Isa. 43:7 – "created for His glory"

Rom. 3:23 – "all have sinned and come short of the glory of God"

Col. 1:27 – "this is the mystery, Christ in you, the hope of glory."

How do we appropriate the risen life of Jesus and live by that life?

John 1:12,13 – "As many as received Him, to them He gave the right to become children of God, even to those who believe in His name, who were born, not of blood nor of the will of the flesh nor of the will of man, but of God."

John 3:16 – "God so loved the world that He gave His only begotten Son, that whoever believes into Him should not perish, but have everlasting life."

Gal. 3:26 – "You are sons of God through faith in Christ Jesus"

Eph. 2:8-10 – "For by grace you have been saved through faith; and that not of yourselves, it is the gift of god; not as a result of works, so that no one may boast. For we are His workmanship, created in Christ Jesus for good works, which God prepared beforehand so that we would walk in them."

We appropriate and receive Christ's resurrection life by FAITH – our receptivity of His activity. This is a reality that only He can enact; not something we do.

YES, Christians will participate in a future resurrection of their bodies, experiencing the perpetuity of life we have in Jesus. Continuum.

I Cor. 15:20-22 – "now Christ has been raised from the dead, the first fruits of those who are asleep. [21] For since by a man *came* death, by a man also *came* the resurrection of the dead. For as in Adam all die, so also in Christ all will be made alive.

I Cor. 15:42-46 – "So also is the resurrection of the dead. It is sown a perishable *body*, it is raised an imperishable *body*; it is sown in dishonor, it is raised in glory; it is sown in weakness, it is raised in power; it is sown a natural body, it is raised a spiritual body. If there is a natural body, there is also a spiritual body. So also, it is written, "The first man, Adam, became a living soul." The last Adam *became* a life-giving spirit. However, the spiritual is not first, but the natural; then the spiritual."

I Cor. 15:54-57 – "But when this perishable will have put on [b]the imperishable, and this mortal will have put on immortality, then will come about the saying that is written, "Death is swallowed up in victory. O death, where is your victory? O death, where is your sting?" The sting of death is sin, and the power of sin is the law; but thanks be to God, who gives us the victory through our Lord Jesus Christ."

John 6:44,54 – "I will raise Him up on the last day."

II Cor. 4:14 – "He who raised the Lord Jesus will raise us also with Jesus..."

Phil. 3:11 – "that I may attain to the resurrection from the dead."

It is important to differentiate between the remedial work of Jesus Christ to put to death the consequences of our sin, as differentiated from the restorative work of Christ to restore the divine life to human spirits.

This difference has also been referred to as the "Objective work of Christ" and the "Subjective work of Christ."

The Christ who lived in history at the beginning of the first century A.D. is the same Christ of our subjective experience in every age.

Christianity is participating in the continuity of the life of the risen Lord Jesus, now and forever.

John Scheffler --

Though Christ a thousand times in Bethlehem be born,
If He's not born in you, your soul is still forlorn.
Though Christ a thousand times be raised on Easter
morn, if He's not raised in you, your soul is still forlorn.

ENDNOTES

1 Josephus, *The Works of Josephus: Complete and Unabridged. The Antiquities of the Jews.* Book 18, chapter 3, section 3. Peabody: Hendrickson Publishers, Inc. 1987. pg. 480.

Resurrection NOW

I have observed that when the topic of "resurrection" is considered in Christian teaching, it is usually used to emphasize "Resurrection **THEN**" (in the past), or "Resurrection **WHEN**" (in the future), but seldom to emphasize "Resurrection **NOW**" (in the present).

There is such a tendency in the teaching of Christian religion to emphasize the *past* and the *future*, to the neglect of the *present*. Often there is an emphasis on the fact that our *past* sins are forgiven, and our *future* destiny is assured, but the *present* provision for living the Christian life is sidestepped. Our *past* is forgiven; our *future* is assured; but the *present* is the "pits"! It seems that the best that the Christian religion can offer is that we are just "hanging on for dear life" on the rickety roller-coaster ride of present existence, hoping for a rapture to relieve us from the ruckus, or awaiting our death in order to depart into our heavenly destiny.

I am not content with a religious message that has both ends covered (past and future), but does not have an adequate message of hope and provision for the **NOW** – the present! A message of *past remedy* and *future reward,* without the fullness of a *present reality* that allows one to live life to the fullness day-by-day and moment-by-moment in Jesus Christ is a static and sterile message of what "has been" and what "will be" without any NOW. It is but a religious sandwich with nothing in the middle – no meat – no substance! It is a religious method that leaves a vacuous void right where we need it most – right

NOW! It is a message that leaves people in the "black hole" of religion, constantly compressed into the conformity of restrictive performance, hoping that we won't get "left behind," and forever sucked-in to the vortex of religious subterfuge of methodology for living.

The "good news" of the Christian gospel is that the Resurrection-Life of the risen and living Lord Jesus is a vital and dynamic presence with the Christian that provides a centrifugal action that forces the character of Christ out into Christian behavior – right **NOW** – in every circumstance of our present lives. Resurrection **NOW**!

Prior to considering the Biblical basis of "Resurrection **NOW**," we are going to document the legitimacy of "Resurrection **THEN**" and "Resurrection **WHEN**." We must not deny or denigrate the veracity of the historical resurrection of Jesus Christ, or the expected resurrection of our bodies in the future, but the really exciting part is "Resurrection **NOW**."

Resurrection THEN

The historical event and fact of the resurrection of Jesus Christ from the dead was foretold and predicted beforehand:

> Matt. 16:13-21 - "Jesus began to show His disciples that He must go to Jerusalem, and suffer many things, and be killed, and be raised up on the third day.
>
> Matt. 20:17-19 - "the Son of Man will be condemned to death...and on the third day He will be raised up."
>
> Mk. 8:31 - "He began to teach them that the Son of Man must suffer and be rejected, and be killed, and after three days rise again."

Mk. 9:31 - "Son of Man delivered into hands of men, and they will kill Him, and He will rise three days later."

Mk. 10:34 - "They will mock Him and spit on Him, and scourge Him and kill Him, and three days later He will rise again."

Lk. 24:7 - "Remember how He spoke, saying the Son of Man must be crucified and on the third day risen again."

Jesus also alluded to His coming resurrection by using different analogies:

Temple analogy: Jn. 2:19-21 - "Destroy this temple and in three days I will raise it up."

Analogy of Jonah: Matt. 12:39-41 - "As Jonah was three days in the belly of the sea monster, so will the Son of Man be three days in the heart of the earth."

Analogy of the wheat seed: Jn. 12:24 - "a grain of wheat falls into the earth and dies, but if it dies, it bears much fruit."

The historical record of the physical resurrection of Jesus is recorded in each of the four gospels: Matt. 27:62 – 28:7; Mk. 16:1-13; Lk. 24:1-12; Jn. 20:1-31. Paul also verifies the historicity of the physical resurrection of Jesus in I Cor. 15:1-9.

The physical resurrection of Jesus was a supernatural miracle. The singularity of this miracle is the basis of much of the apologetic emphasis in Christian religion, whereby they attempt to:

(1) prove resurrection historically

(2) prove deity of Christ thereby

Apologetics has its place, but must not be an end in itself.

The resurrection of Jesus Christ **THEN** is historical data.

Implications of the historical data explicate the reality of Christian gospel.

Christianity is more than just an historical society to remember the historical details of Jesus' birth, death, and resurrection.

Resurrection WHEN

In the "resurrection chapter" of I Corinthians 15, Paul makes an extended effort to demonstrate that "Resurrection **WHEN**" is based upon "Resurrection **THEN**."

Historical context of I Corinthians 15 - Corinthians Christians enamored with their "spirituality" (I Cor. 12-14) in context of "spiritual gifts." They had developed a "triumphalism" wherein they thought they had "arrived" at the summit of spirituality, and had no concern for anything in the future.

Paul counters this "triumphalism" by tying the historical resurrection of Jesus Christ to the future expectation of a heavenly resurrection of the body for Christians.

The issue is a similarity of resurrected re-embodiment (which Paul addresses again in II Corinthians 5). The issue is NOT a similarity in the physicality of resurrection. The physically resurrected body of Jesus is NOT necessarily prototypical of the resurrection body of Christians, which is described as a "heavenly body" (15:40), an "imperishable body" (15:42), a "body of glory" (15:43; Phil. 3:21), a "spiritual body" (15:44).

I Cor. 15:12-22 – "Now if Christ is preached, that He has been raised from the dead, how do some among you say that there is no resurrection of the dead? But if there is no resurrection of the dead, not even Christ has been raised; and if Christ has not been raised, then our preaching is vain, your faith also is vain. Moreover we are even found to be false witnesses of God, because we testified against God that He raised Christ, whom He did not raise, if in fact the dead are not raised. For if the dead are not raised, not even Christ has been raised; and if Christ has not been raised, your faith is worthless; you are still in your sins. Then those also who have fallen asleep in Christ have perished. If we have hoped in Christ in this life only, we are of all men most to be pitied."

I Cor. 6:14 - Now God has not only raised the Lord, but will also raise us up through His power."

Jesus had previously referred to "being raised up on the last day"

John 6:40 – "everyone who beholds the Son and believes in Him will have eternal life, and I Myself will raise him up on the last day."

John 6:44 – "No one can come to Me unless the Father who sent Me draws him; and I will raise him up on the last day."

John 6:54 – "He who eats My flesh and drinks My blood has eternal life, and I will raise him up on the last day."

There is indeed a future hope, a future expectation of heavenly resurrection and re-embodiment. But we must not revert to the mind-set of Jewish theology and eschatology, which always perceived things in expectation of "future fulfillment." Christian theology and eschatology, on the other hand, recognized the realized life of Jesus Christ **NOW**, as well as the future expectations. This is the balanced dialectic between the "already" and the "not yet."

The ultimate objective and hope of the Christian gospel is not simply to get to heaven, to have a future residence and changed embodiment. The objective of the Christian gospel is to allow for the restoration of God's life to man in Jesus Christ, allowing His life to be lived out in our behavior **NOW** on the way to heaven. Heaven is but the continuum and perpetuity of the Resurrection-Life or eternal life that we have received in Jesus at spiritual regeneration.

Resurrection NOW

Paul recognized that the "Resurrection **WHEN**" was founded upon the "Resurrection **NOW**."

Phil. 3:11 - "that I may know Him and the power of His resurrection...*in order that* I may attain to the resurrection from the dead."

There is no "Resurrection **WHEN**" if there is no "Resurrection **NOW**" – the future is the continuum of the present **NOW**.

John 11:21-27 - "**I AM** the resurrection and the life." That's a present tense - NOW. Martha was thinking of the "Resurrection WHEN" (vs. 24) and Jesus was directing her to the "Resurrection NOW."

Rom. 1:4 - "Jesus was declared the Son of God with power by the *resurrection* from the dead." The Son of God who had the power to restore spiritual life to mankind

In spiritual regeneration, we are re-lifed with the Resurrection-Life of the risen and living Lord Jesus Christ. By His resurrection and ascension, He has become the "life-giving Spirit" (I Cor. 15:45). "The Lord is the Spirit" (II Cor. 3:17). "The Spirit gives life" (II Cor. 3:6). "If any man does not have the Spirit of Christ, he is none of His" (Rom. 8:9). "In Christ, all can be made alive" (I Cor. 15:22).

John 14:6 - "**I AM** the way, the truth, and the life."

I John 5:12 - "He who has the Son has life; he who does not have the Son of God does not have the life."

To illustrate the initiatory reception of this spiritual, resurrection-life of Jesus, the Bible uses the metaphor of birth.

John 3:1-8 - "You must be born again." (from above).

I Peter 1:3 - "Blessed be the God and Father of our Lord Jesus Christ, who according to His great mercy has caused us to be *born again* to a living hope through the *resurrection* of Jesus Christ from the dead." -- Resurrection prerequisite to receipt of resurrection-life in regeneration.

(Jesus' resurrection from the dead was also referred to as a birth. Acts 13:33 - quotes from Ps. 2:7 - "You are My Son; Today I have begottten You." Cf. Col. 1:18; Rev. 1:5 - Jesus is "first born from the dead"; Rom. 8:29 - "first born among many brethren.")

Christians participate in spiritual re-enactment of Jesus' death and resurrection, as they pass from death to life.

John 5:24,25 - Jesus said, "Truly, truly, I say to you, he who hears My word, and believe Him who sent Me, has eternal life, and does not come into judgment, but has passed out of death into life. Truly, truly, I say to you, an hour is coming and NOW is, when the dead will hear the voice of the Son of God, and those who hear will live"

I John 3:14 - "We know that we have passed out of death into life.'

Rom. 6:3-11 - Paul explains to the Roman Christians that they participate in "Resurrection **NOW**" (with the anticipation of "Resurrection **WHEN**")

Rom. 6:4 - "as Christ was raised from the dead, so we too might walk in newness of life"

Rom. 6:11 - "consider yourselves to be dead to sin, but alive to God in Christ Jesus"

Similarly, in his letter to the Colossians, Paul writes,

Col. 2:12,13 - "you were also *raised up with Him* through faith in the working of God, who raised Him from the dead."

Col. 3:1 - "Therefore if you have been raised up with Christ, keep seeking the things above, where Christ is, seated at the right hand of God.

Col. 3:3,4 - "you have died and your life is hidden with Christ in God. When Christ, *who is our life* (NOW) is revealed, then you also will be revealed with Him in glory (Resurrection WHEN).

Gal. 2:20 - "I have been crucified with Christ; and it is no longer I who lives, but Christ lives in me."

II Cor. 13:5 - "Do you not recognize that Jesus Christ is in you?"

Phil. 1:21 - "For me to live is Christ"

Eph. 2:4-9 - "raised us up with Him" (6)

Eph. 1:18-23 - "surpassing greatness of His (resurrection) power..."

I Cor. 1:24 - "Christ, the power of God"

Phil. 3:7-11 - "that I may know Him and the power of His resurrection" (**NOW**) ...in order that I may attain to the resurrection from the dead" (**WHEN**)

Eph. 3:20 - "Now to Him who is able to do far more abundantly beyond all that we ask or think, according to the power that works with us" (Resurrection power of risen, living Lord Jesus).

Christianity IS the Resurrection-reality of the risen and living Lord Jesus – living within us; living His life out through us. The Resurrection-LIFE of Jesus is the dynamic for everything in the Christian life. That is why Easter – the celebration of the Resurrection **THEN** – is the focal point of the Christian year, as we celebrate Resurrection **NOW**, and look forward to Resurrection **WHEN**.

Resurrection: The Key to Understanding the Gospel

The ancient Egyptians had a form of picture writing which later researchers called hieroglyphics. The word itself is Greek and means "sacred" or "priestly carving."

For decades, centuries, for over a millennium (c. 500 A.D. to 1822 A.D.) no one could decipher the Egyptian hieroglyphic writings. They thought it was a secret code of the priests and that the "key" for understanding was lost forever.

Then, in 1799 some of Napoleon's soldiers found what was called "The Rosetta Stone" near the mouth of the Nile River. This stone had the same inscription written in three different languages: Egyptian hieroglyphics, Egyptian demotic, and Greek. It still took twenty-three years, until 1822, when the Frenchman, Francois Champollion, discovered the "key" to unlock the mysterious symbols and translate the hieroglyphic script.

The gospel is like hieroglyphics to many people today; somewhat like a "sacred carving" that no one can understand. For years and years people have known about the gospel, paid homage to the gospel, celebrated the gospel, but they have often not understood what it meant. It is as if the gospel is a secret code of the priests, and the "key" to understanding has been lost.

It is time that we find the Resurrection stone, and discover the "key" to unlock these religious mysteries, to interpret the gospel as it was intended. The resurrection is a far more important discovery for mankind than the Rosetta Stone was to Egyptologists. The resurrection is the "key" to understanding the gospel and its life-import for all peoples.

There are many Biblical concepts and words that are just hieroglyphic symbols, just obscure religious carvings in "Christian religion" today. Their meaning, for the most part, has been lost for centuries, for over a millennium. The "key" to understanding these important Biblical truths is a proper perspective of the resurrection.

The concept of resurrection must first be decoded. The resurrection is not just an historical event, not just a theological truth. The resurrection is a living, personal reality in the Person of Jesus Christ. Jesus said, "I AM the resurrection and the life." (John 11:25)

Jesus was indeed raised from the dead historically on that "first day of the week." The theological significance of "life out of death" and eventual bodily resurrection is truly important. The present significance of the resurrection is recognized when Christians understand that the risen Lord Jesus ascended to heaven, and the very resurrection-life of Jesus was poured out on Pentecost to dwell in the spirits of Christian people. That spiritual reality, the indwelling of the living Lord Jesus, the dynamic function of His resurrection-life in and through our lives, is the essence of the gospel. Jesus, the "resurrection and the life," is living out His resurrection-life in us; the Christ-life expressed in the Christian.

Many of the "things of God" remain hieroglyphics to many Christian people because the reality of the resurrection-life of Jesus is not applied to Biblical truth. What we will do in this study is to take a list of some of the "things of God" from Scripture (not exhaustive), and note how they remain hieroglyphic symbols until we understand them in the light of the dynamic resurrection-life of Jesus.

Image of God

The interpretation of the "image of God" remains in hieroglyphic symbol for many Christian expositors. A study of the commentators and systematic theologians can produce a list of over twenty-five different explanations (ex. physical stature, trichotomy, spirituality, intelligence, emotion, volition, personality, moral ability, masculinity, eternality, creativity, etc.) of the meaning of the "image of God."

From a perspective of the dynamic of Christ's resurrection-life, we have the "key" to understand that "Christ is the image of God." (cf. Col. 1:15; II Cor. 4:4). Jesus Christ by His resurrection-life in the Christian allows the invisible character of God to be made visible in the behavior of man unto the glory of God. When we become a Christian, we are restored with the possibility of bearing the image of God (Gen. 1:27; Col. 3:10), because Jesus Christ, the "image of God" is the One who makes God visible. The character of God is imaged, visaged, in our behavior as the risen Lord Jesus lives out His life through us.

Life of God

So often the life of God remains a hieroglyphic carving for it is viewed with a separated concept whereby God is "Wholly Other," or the life of God is something we come into contact with after we die physically; or the life of God is an ideal that we strive for here on earth.

Jesus said, "I AM the resurrection and the life" (John 11:25); "I AM the way, the truth and the life" (John 14:6). "Just as the Father has life in Himself, even so He gave to the Son to have life in Himself." (John 5:26). "In Him was life and the life was the light of men" (John 1:4). The risen Lord Jesus is the life of God having come to live in us and to empower His character to be lived out through us. "The life of Jesus manifested in our mortal flesh" (II Cor. 4:10,11). "Christ is our life" (Col. 3:4). The resurrection is the "key" to understanding how the life of Jesus functions in us day by day and moment by moment as Christians.

Law of God

The Law of God is considered by many to be but behavioral regulations carved in stone, as indeed they were on the tablets given to Moses on Mt. Sinai. Codes of conduct full of "thou shalts" and "thou shalt nots" – obedient adherence to which all men are expected to conform – this is the moralizing and ethical expectation that religion projects concerning the Law.

Understanding the resurrection-life of Jesus Christ allows us to decipher the meaning of the Law symbol. The Law has been written in our hearts and upon our minds" (Heb. 8:10; 10:16), because the living Lord Jesus is the One who is the expression of the character of God, and He is the dynamic to express such in our behavior by the grace of God. Thus, He fulfills both the essential and the functional purposes of the law. Jesus Christ is the living Torah in every Christian. He is the Law-giver and the Law-keeper. The regulatory concepts of the law are annulled. Jesus Christ is the end of the Law (Rom. 10:4), the fulfilment of the Law (Matt. 5:17). Christians are "no longer under the Law, but under grace" (Rom. 6:14,15).

Will of God

The meaning of the "will of God" is often imbedded in precise expectations that God has pre-determined exacting plans for each individual; that there is a plotted course prescribed for every action of our lives. Many people spend much of their time mulling over every detail in their lives trying to figure out the meaning of "God's will" for their lives – much like the Egyptologists who tried to figure out the meaning of the hieroglyphics year after year for centuries.

The "will of God" is not a prescription; it is a Person. The will of God is Jesus Christ, restored to dwell in the spirits of created mankind and allowed to live out His life and character in our behavior, by the grace activity of His resurrection-life. The will of God is to be filled with the Spirit of Christ (Eph. 5:17,18). The resurrection-life of Jesus is the "will of God" for every Christian.

Israel of God

Just as hieroglyphics were pictures with a meaning, in like manner God used pictorial representation to explain what He intended. One of God's pictorial preliminaries was the nation of Israel. As a physical people and nation, they represented the spiritual peoples who would receive the resurrection-life of Jesus Christ; people who had striven with God and surrendered to God and in whom God now rules (Gen. 32:28; 35:10). Thus it is that Christians are now the "Israel of God" (Gal. 6:16), though not descended from physical Israel (Rom. 9:6). Christ rules as risen Lord in the lives of the holy nation (I Peter 2:9) of Christian Israel, that is all Christians who have received His resurrection-life by faith and are living by faith.

Kingdom of God

The "kingdom of God" is another figure that God used to pre-figure His intent. The Jews conceived of the kingdom of God as a nationalistic kingdom with a Jewish king in the realm of Palestine. There are still Zionist expectations in Judeo-Christian religion today, focusing on a futuristic physical millennial kingdom in Palestine.

Jesus said, "My kingdom is not of this world (John 18:36); the kingdom of God is within you (Luke 17:21). The resurrection is the "key" to ascertain the spiritual intent of the kingdom of God. To Nicodemus, Jesus explained that "unless you are born again you cannot see the kingdom of God (John 3:3,5), for Christians are "born again to a living hope through the resurrection of Jesus Christ from the dead" (I Peter 1:23). By the indwelling of the resurrection-life of Jesus Christ "we reign in life through Jesus Christ" (Rom. 5:17) as Jesus, the "King of Kings" reigns in the kingdom of our hearts in "righteousness, peace and joy" (Rom. 14:17).

People of God

God's desire for a "people of God" is often misrepresented by factors of racism, nationalism and religion. The "people of God" are not a privileged few chosen by arbitrary selection with exclusivist rights concerning which they can boast with pompous pride. The Hebrew people of the old covenant were called the "people of God" merely as a pictorial pre-figuring to point to the spiritual reality of the "people of God" in Jesus Christ, i.e. to Christians. Hosea explained this so graphically by naming his son Lo-ammi meaning "not My people" (Hosea 1:9; 2:23), to which Paul refers in identifying Christians as the "people of God" (Rom. 9:25,26). Ezekiel (Ezek. 37:23,27) and Jeremiah (Jere. 31:1,33) both prophesied of the time of fulfilment when by the resurrection of Jesus the life of God would be restored to men and they would be the "people of God" in Jesus Christ. Paul (II Cor. 6:16); Titus 2:14), Peter (I Peter 2:9,10) and the writer to the Hebrews (Heb. 8:10) all refer to this intended understanding of the "people of God," the people who live by the resurrection-life of Jesus Christ.

Love of God

The "love of God" is often depicted in such metaphorical figuration as to be covered in syrupy sentimentalism. Yes, "God is love" (I John 4:8,16), but this does not override His justice or even His wrath. God's love is not just an introductory compassion that moved Him to "so love the world and give His only begotten Son" (John 3:16) in order to redeem man and get man "off the hook."

By the resurrection we understand that the love of God is received, experienced and expressed only by the indwelling presence of the risen Lord Jesus. "The love of God has been poured out within our hearts through the Holy Spirit who was given to us" (Rom. 5:5). The "love of God surpasses knowledge" (Eph. 3:19) and "nothing is able to separate us from the love of God which is in Christ Jesus our Lord" (Rom. 8:39). "If we love one another, God abides in us" (I John 4:12) and the love of God expressed through us is the "fruit of the Spirit" (Gal. 5:22). The active love of God in the Christian is but the functioning of the resurrection-life of Jesus in us.

Word of God

The "Word of God" is another concept often obscured within Christian religion today. Some interpret "Word of God" to be God's decrees and pronouncements. Others explain that it is a law or principle that God employed for expressed creativity. The predominant theory is that the "Word of God" is the written text of the Bible.

Once again, the "key" to understanding the "Word of God" is only through the recognition of the resurrection of Jesus Christ. Jesus is the "Word of God!" "In the beginning was the Word, and the Word was with God, and the Word was God" (John 1:1. "The Word became flesh and dwelt among us" (John 1:14). By His resurrection Jesus became the ever-living Word, to express the divine resurrection-life in Christians. Christians are people who have "received the Word of God" (Acts 11:1; I Thess. 2:13), i.e. Jesus; who have been "born again through the living and active Word of God" (I Peter 1:23), and in whom the "word of God abides" (I John 2:14) and is "living and active" (Heb. 4:12). Jesus Christ, the risen and living "Word of God," expresses the life of God in us by His resurrection-life.

Gospel of God

Even the concept of "gospel" is encrypted in the creeds and codes of religion. The historical narratives of Jesus' incarnated life are referred to as "gospels," and for some that is the entire meaning of "gospel." For others, the "gospel" is but a "salvation recipe" or the compilation of definitive doctrines dogmatically determined with theological precision to comprise an orthodox belief-system. Thus, some have referred to "the gospel according to Jesus" or the apostles or others (cf. John MacArthur).

The gospel is Jesus! Jesus is the "good news"! The gospel is the good news of the dynamic life of the risen Lord Jesus restored to indwell man and function in man unto the glory of God. Christians are "called through the gospel" (II Thess. 2:14), "begotten through the gospel" (I Cor. 4:15); they "participate in the gospel" (Phil. 1:5); they share in "the hope of the gospel" (Col. 1:23). The gospel is the "gospel of Christ" (Rom. 15:19; II Cor. 10:14; Phil. 1:23; II Thess. 1:8). The resurrection is the "key" to understanding the gospel as the dynamic of the life of the risen Lord Jesus. That is the only "good news" there is for man.

Salvation of God

When the significance of something so crucial as salvation is suppressed in the symbolism of religion, it is a sad indictment upon those who are supposed to be interpreters and expositors. Salvation is often cast as a commodity, an eternal life package, a ticket to heaven; some "thing" that can be found, dispensed, acquired, that one can "get" or "possess." Salvation is portrayed as a fire-insurance policy making one safe from hell, a political liberation making one safe from oppressors, a new-thought pattern making one safe from erroneous thinking.

Jesus is the Savior! Jesus is salvation! Jesus is "the source of eternal salvation" (Heb. 5:9). There is "salvation in no other name" (Acts 4:12). The "salvation of God" is made available to all men in Christ (Luke 3:6; Acts 28:28). "For by grace are we saved through faith" (Eph. 2:5,8). The salvation that is in Christ (II Tim. 2:10) is revealed only by the resurrection of Jesus Christ. Salvation is the process whereby the Savior makes us safe from spiritual abuse, misuse and dysfunction in order to function as intended by the resurrection-life of Jesus Christ. Salvation must never be disconnected from the on-going work of the Savior, from the "saving life of Christ" (Rom. 5:10).

Blessing of God

The "blessing of God" has been obscured by those who think only of "counting their many blessings" of material things and pleasant situations, by those who interpret God's "blessing" as numerically calculable results, productivity and miracles, and by those who feel that God's "blessing" is a subjective sensation, a tickle of emotional excitement.

In the old covenant there was much reference to blessings and curses (cf. Deut. 28), but they were but typological indicators that Jesus Christ would take upon Himself the curses and become to us all the blessings of God. Peter explains that "God raised up His Son and sent Him to bless" us (Acts 3:26), and that because Jesus is the seed of Abraham, "by whom all the families of the earth are blessed" (Acts 3:25; Gal. 3:14). "God has blessed us with every spiritual blessing in heavenly places in Christ Jesus" (Eph. 1:3). We have "the fullness of the blessing of Christ" (Rom. 15:29). The resurrection-life of Jesus Christ is God's "good word" (*eu-logia*), blessing and God's activity in us.

Truth of God

"What is truth?" asked Pilate (John 18:38), and many have been trying to find the clue to sorting-out truth ever since. The "truth of God" is often left encoded in propositional truth statements. Truth is regarded as logical accuracy of sentential statements in accord with the evidence available. Thus men regard their premises, their precepts, their principles as truth.

The "truth of God" is personified in Jesus Christ, who said, "I AM the way, the truth and the life" (John 14:6). "Truth is in Jesus" (Eph. 4:21); He is "full of grace and truth" (John 1:14). It is by the availability of the resurrection-life of Jesus that what Jesus promised is made real in our lives: "You shall know the truth, and the truth shall set you free" (John 8:32), later explaining that "the Son shall set you free" (John 8:36). Jesus, as the living Word is truth (John 17:17). The Spirit of Christ is the truth of God (I John 5:7). The resurrection reality of the risen and living Lord Jesus is the "truth of God" that He wants all men to know and experience.

Power of God

The "power of God" is often concealed in the machinations of Christian religion. The hierarchical powers of ecclesiasticism exercise their authority and control in strong-arm tactics of coercion. Other religionists develop a "power-theology" that stereotypes God in demonstrations of miraculous power-manifestations. The word of God to Zerubbabel was, "'Not by might, nor by power, but by My Spirit,' says the Lord of hosts" (Zech. 4:6). Jesus told the Sadducean religionists, "you do not understand the scriptures or the power of God" (Matt. 22:29).

Jesus was "declared to be the Son of God with power by the resurrection from the dead" (Rom. 1:4). "Christ is the power of God" (I Cor. 1:24). When the risen Lord Jesus dwells in us, we have "the surpassing greatness of the power of God" (II Cor. 4:7), "working in us" (Eph. 3:20). The "power of Christ dwells in us" (II Cor. 12:9). The "gift of grace is given to us according to the working of His power" (Eph. 3:7), and we are "strengthened with power through His Spirit in the inner man" (Eph. 3:18). That is why Paul desired to know "the power of His resurrection" (Phil. 3:10). The resurrection reveals the power of God.

Grace of God

Oh the tragedy of allowing the "grace of God" to remain statically chiselled in the hieroglyphic forms of religion. Grace is often depicted as merely the "undeserved favor of God," nothing more than the graciousness, mercy or pity of God. Yes, that is the extent of the understanding of grace in the old covenant, because the Hebrew language did not even have a word that corresponded with the New Testament concept of "grace." Yet Christian religion has allowed grace to remain solidified and static as merely the "threshold factor" of redemptive grace, as typified in the popular acrostic: God's Redemption At Christ's Expense.

It is in the light of the resurrection of Jesus Christ that we see that grace is the dynamic activity of God in the life of the risen Lord Jesus. "Grace is realized through Jesus Christ" (John 1:17); the "grace of God was given to us in Christ Jesus" (I Cor. 1:4); "grace was freely bestowed on us in the Beloved" (Eph. 1:6). "The grace of God has appeared (in Jesus Christ), bringing salvation to all men" (Titus 2:11). We have an identity as "Christians", participating in the resurrection-life of Jesus, only by the grace of God (I Cor. 15:10). The Christian life, the life of the risen Lord Jesus lived out in us, is only lived by the dynamic of God's grace. As Christians, we do not want to nullify such (Gal. 2:21), but to continue in the grace of God (Acts 13:43) which is ever sufficient (II Cor. 12:9), and that to the very end (Rev. 22:21). The grace of the resurrection-life of Jesus is the essence of the Christian gospel.

Church of God

The understanding of the "church of God" is often hidden in false impressions. Some view it as a building, others as a "worship experience" or a meeting, others as a social grouping of like-minded ideologues, and still others as a political institution.

The resurrection of Jesus Christ defines the "church of God" as those who are "called out" to be all God intends them to be by His activity of resurrection-life in and through them. Jesus Christ is the "head of the Body, the church" (Eph. 5:23; Col. 1:18,24). The church is the "Body of Christ" (Eph. 4:12), the collective expression of the life of the risen Lord Jesus, the resurrection community, the "church of the living God" (I Tim. 3:15). The world is supposed to see the out-working of the life of Jesus Christ on earth today as the resurrection-life of Jesus functions in the interpersonal relationships of Christian peoples.

These are but a few of the "things of God," the significance of which are only explained and interpreted by the dynamic of the resurrection-life of Jesus Christ. We could go on to decode the concepts of the righteousness of God, the wisdom of God, the peace of God, the glory of God, the city of God, the way of God, the covenant of God, the house of God, the temple of God, the holiness of God, the sovereignty of God and many more. The "deep things of God" (I Cor. 2:10-KJV) that remain so mysterious, hidden, concealed and unintelligible in Christian religion, must be decoded and deciphered by the resurrection of Jesus Christ.

The realization of the resurrection is the "key" that unlocks the revelation of God from the hieroglyphics of religious terminology. The resurrection reveals that the message of God made available by God's grace and written down so many centuries ago is that Jesus Christ is "the summing up of all spiritual things" (Eph. 1:10). Everything that God has to give is made available in the resurrection-life of Jesus Christ.

The gospel is not a series of encoded pictograms of doctrinal truth obfuscating what God intended to express. The gospel is Jesus Christ, "the resurrection and the life" (John 11:25). Christianity is Christ!

THE LOGIC OF RESURRECTION

Many people regard the resurrection of Jesus Christ as illogical, as did the philosophers in the Areopagus on Mars Hill in Athens, who "when they heard of the resurrection from the dead, began to sneer" (Acts 17:32). Since it does not fit within the predetermined parameters of acceptable criteria based upon empirical evidence observable by sensory perception, those demanding naturalistic scientific explanation in deductive and inductive logical forms often reject the resurrection as not documentable and beyond the bounds of human reason. They seldom recognize that they have self-limited the parameters of their evidence and their logical reasoning to a space-time context, disallowing and eschewing the vast realm of spiritual, supernatural and divine phenomena. How logical and scientific are they who would disallow evidence that does not fit and conform to their predetermined and pre-formed parameters of observation and conclusion? Do they really seek the *scientia* of complete knowledge?

The objective of this study is to consider the logic of the resurrection of Jesus using several logical categories that reveal the reality, rationale, and personal renewal of the resurrection. Though some of these categories can be submitted to the courts of visible history and visible observation, the particular category of ontological, present experience of the resurrection that will be the primary focus of this study is singularly rooted in the divine action of God beyond the realm of naturalistic explanation. We recognize in advance, therefore, that the naturalistic scoffers will not be convinced by our logical categories, despite how we might describe such (cf. Acts 13:41).

Chrono*logical* consideration of the resurrection

All considerations of Christian resurrection must commence in the *chronos* of time and history. The Greek word *chronos* referred to sequential historical time. The resurrection of Jesus from the dead on that first Easter morning was an historical event in the sequence of His life, death, burial, resurrection, ascension, and continued manifestation.

The varied historical narratives of the four gospels record the initial details and witnesses of the resurrection of Jesus Christ from the tomb (cf. Matt. 28:1-10; Mk. 16:1-13; Lk. 24:1-12; Jn. 20:1-18). In his historical sequel, Luke records that Jesus "also presented Himself alive to His disciples, after His suffering, by many convincing proofs, appearing to them over forty days, and speaking of the things concerning the kingdom of God" (Acts 1:3). In the great chapter on "resurrection," Paul bases his message of the gospel on the historicity of the resurrection: "For I delivered to you as of first importance what I also received, that Christ died for our sins according to the Scriptures, and that He was buried, and He was raised on the third day according to the Scriptures, and that He appeared to Cephas, then to the twelve. After that He appeared to more than five hundred brethren at one time, most of whom remain until now, but some have fallen asleep; then He appeared to James, then to all the apostles; and last of all, as it were to one untimely born, He appeared to me also." (I Cor. 15:4-8).

These chronological accounts of the witnesses of the resurrected Jesus provide the primary historical evidence of Jesus' resurrection from the dead. The historical veracity of the resurrection is fundamentally and foundationally important to the Christian faith. It prevents religion from fashioning a mere phantasm of subjective projection concerning the concept of resurrection, as if it were but a mythological or mystical "raising of one's consciousness" or other psychological phenomenon of raising expectations, incentives, well-being, etc. The historicity of the resurrection event roots the divine action in the *chronos* of time and space. This has been the basis for traditional historical apologetics whereby Christians have attempted to defend their faith by explaining the evidences for the existence and resurrection of Jesus Christ in history. While beneficial for establishing chronological historicity, it must be understood that the historical event of the physical resurrection of Jesus served as the stage setting for the eternal dynamic of divine resurrection.

On the basis of the chronological consideration of the resurrection, we can affirm that "Jesus was raised from the dead." But Jesus' statement, "I AM the resurrection..." (Jn. 11:25) has limited meaning in this chronological context. Though Jesus made that statement in a particular time and place in the past, the chronological consideration of past events in historical time is not the logical venue for evaluating the every-present tense of "I AM the resurrection..."

Theo*logical* consideration of the resurrection

Christian theology seeks to consider the resurrection by evaluating and explaining the historical resurrection-event in terms of God's objective and on-going divine work. It is the formulation of interpretive data concerning the meaning of the historical resurrection of Jesus Christ, evaluating the purpose of the resurrection in God's redemptive plan, and explaining the implications of Christ's resurrection for Christian individuals in the future. Theological considerations have usually subdivided, therefore, into (1) the *soteriological* consideration of the resurrection, and (2) the *eschatological* consideration of the resurrection.

Soteriological considerations have usually addressed the resurrection as the divine solution to the crucifixion, whereby God brought Jesus to life again out of death. In His death on the cross Jesus vicariously and substitutionally took upon Himself the death consequences of man's sin, and by His resurrection Jesus secures the benefits of His redemptive action. Indeed, it is true that there would be no forgiveness of sins if Christ had not been raised from the dead (I Cor. 15:17), and the purpose of His being raised was for our justification (Rom. 4:25). But Protestant theology, as a whole, has so tended to objectify the status and standing of the Christian's benefits of imputed life and righteousness, to the extent that it becomes nothing more than an academic and cerebral reckoning of a heavenly transaction that has little or no bearing on the life that we live here and now. The personal and subjective implications of the resurrection have been eschewed in an overreaction to the "infused grace" theological formulations of Roman Catholicism.

Eschatological considerations of the resurrection seek to explain, as Paul did in I Corinthians 15 that the resurrection of Jesus Christ was the prototype of the eventual resurrection that all Christians can expect after death. The fact that Jesus was raised from the dead is evidence that those who are identified with Christ as Christians also have the hope of life after death. "Christ has been raised from the dead, the first fruits of those who are asleep" (I Cor. 15:20) in death. "He who raised up the Lord Jesus will raise us also with Jesus" (II Cor. 4:14) in "the resurrection of the dead" (Phil. 3:11). The eschatological considerations of theology attempt to give explanation of the expectation of the future bodily resurrection of Christians based upon the historical event of Christ's resurrection

Theological considerations of the resurrection necessarily deal with impersonal data interpreting the facts of history in an epistemological explanation. Christian theology explains that "the meaning of the resurrection is..., and the logical results of the resurrection will be..., but seldom does theology proceed to consider or explain the personal and present implications of the resurrection-dynamic of the life of the Lord Jesus dwelling within and functioning through the receptive Christian. Jesus' statement, "I AM the resurrection and the life" (Jn. 11:25) is an essentially personal and present-tense declaration of the Personal dynamic of His resurrection-life that exceeds the usual impersonal considerations of theology. Despite the limited attempts to explain "union with Christ" theologically, the logical explanations must be transcended, and each individual must experience the resurrection-life of the risen Lord Jesus personally and spiritually if they are ever to understand the full implications of Jesus' resurrection.

Onto*logical* consideration of the resurrection

The ontological consideration of the resurrection goes beyond chronological and theological categories. If Resurrection remains in the logic of chronology and theology, then it remains the stale data of history and theology, which becomes the basis of static and dead religion.

The term "ontological" is derived from two Greek words: the Greek word *ontos* is the word for "being", and the word *logos* is the word for "word", from which we get the English word "logic". In the Greek language *ontos* is the genitive, singular, present participle of the Greek verb *eimi* which means "to be". Ontological, therefore, refers to the "understanding of being", and more particularly to the experiential recognition of the Being of God in action.

Protestant theology, as a whole, has tended to emphasize a redemption-theology, to the neglect of resurrection-theology. As such it is objectified to the neglect of the experiential.

Personified resurrection. The logic of the personal Being of God in man by the person and activity of the Spirit of the risen and living Lord Jesus in the Christian.

Jn. 11:25,26 - "I AM the resurrection and the life; he who believes in Me shall live even if he dies, and everyone who lives and believes in Me shall never die." (personal - "I"; present - "AM"; dynamic - "resurrection"; vital - "life.")

Jesus never says, "I AM the cross," or "I AM the crucifixion." The Cross and crucifixion are the remedial action of God on man's behalf, and can only be considered historically and theologically. The Cross cannot be considered ontologically, because death by crucifixion is the termination of "being." (This does not mean that the idea of "death" cannot be experientially and subjectively considered in the "death of old man.")

I AM the resurrection! "I AM" is the first person, singular indicative of the verb "to be." (In Greek, the word *ontos* is the word for Being, and the basis of "ontological"). When the Jews heard this repeated declaration of Jesus: I AM the way, the truth, and the life (Jn. 14:6); I AM the good shepherd (Jn. 10:11,14); I AM the door (Jn. 10:7); Before Abraham was, I AM (Jn. 8:58); I AM the light of the world (Jn. 8:12); I AM the bread of life (Jn. 6:35); I AM speaks to you (Jn. 4:26), they would inevitably have thought of the name of God. They would have thought back to Moses and the narrative in Exodus 3:13,14 - "Moses said to God, 'Behold, I am going to the sons of Israel, and I shall say to them, 'The God of your fathers has sent me to you.' Now they may say to me, "What is His name?' What shall I say to them?' And God said to Moses, "I AM who I AM;" and He said, "Thus you shall say to the sons of Israel, "I AM has sent me to you." The Hebrew name of God, Yahweh (*YHWH*) (from which we get English "Jehovah") is expressed in this revelation of God as "I AM who I AM." The Hebrew name of God was considered unpronounceable and so reverent as to remain unspoken. *YHWH* was mere breath sound.

So, when Jesus came pronouncing Himself as "I AM the resurrection and the life" (Jn. 11:26), the Jews considered such as blasphemy of the name of God. The *ego eimi* pronouncement in Greek was identified with the *YHWH* name of God in Hebrew. Jesus' "I AM" pronouncements were considered to be equivalent to saying, "I AM - GOD." Which indeed, He was saying: "I AM the resurrection-life of God." "I AM the life of God restored to man to make man man as God intended man to be." "I AM the basis of functional humanity by the restoration of the presence of the divine dynamic of God in man." "I AM the God who recreates humanity by the restoration of resurrection-life; MY life in man." "I AM the resurrection - the restoration of Gold's life to man."

That was His claim, and this begins to reveal the Ontological understanding of Resurrection – the Personified resurrection-life of God in Jesus Christ.

We will be considering several quotations from a most enlightening book by Walter Kunneth, *The Theology of the Resurrection*, London: SCM Press, 1965.

Kunneth (211) - "The New Testament knows of no ontology save the resurrection ontology." (The Being of Christian "being" derives only from the Being of Jesus Christ. It does not derive from an alleged inherent or intrinsic human "being" capable of generating, activating, performing or "doing" works that God should look upon as being acceptable."

Our interpretation of the historical event of the physical resurrection of Jesus must go beyond the theological explanation of redemption and future glorification. We must understand what it means to experience Resurrection, as the personal Being of the Resurrected One indwells the Christian and activates his behavior. The resurrection-Life of the risen and living Lord Jesus, by His Spirit, "comes into being" and functions within the Christian. This is the dynamic essence of Christianity. HE is the reality of Christianity. Christianity IS Christ!

This ontological "coming into being" of the Christ-life in the Christian, is figuratively expressed in the New Testament as "new birth" or "being born again." In like manner as Jesus "came into being" again, life out of death, in the historical, physical resurrection event ("begotten of God" - Acts 13:33), He becomes the "first-born of many brethren" (Rom. 8:29) who will likewise "come into being" in resurrection-life. This connection of resurrection and regeneration, the historical resurrection event being the prerequisite to spiritual regeneration, is expressed by Peter when he writes that we are "born again to a living hope through the resurrection of Jesus Christ from the dead" (I Peter 1:3). The very ontological Being of the risen Lord Jesus is made available to mankind by His resurrection, whereby having taken our deserved death in crucifixion He makes available His resurrection-life to enliven men spiritually, and that in order to function in expression of His Life and character.

In that regenerative "coming into being" with Christ's resurrection-life, Christians are depicted as experiencing a co-crucifixion and co-resurrection with Jesus. The old spiritual identity as an "old man" (Rom. 6:6; Eph. 4:22; Col. 3:9) is terminated in a manner that correlates to the death of Jesus Christ on the cross. The old identity passes away when we become a new creature (II Cor. 5:17) in Christ, and as a "new man" (Eph. 4:24; Col. 3:10) we are united in the likeness of Christ's resurrection (Rom. 6:4,5). Taking humanity unto Himself in both crucifixion and resurrection, we were "raised up with Him" (Eph. 2:6; Col. 3:1) "through faith in the working of God, who raised Him from the dead" (Col. 2:12). In the regenerative overwhelming of our spirit with the Spirit of Christ (cf. Rom. 8:9,16), we are raised to newness of life (Rom. 6:4), which is His resurrection-life indwelling our spirit. We are spiritually "joined to Him who was raised from the dead" (Rom. 7:4).

(The historical solidarity enacted at the cross as we were "crucified with Christ" and "raised with Christ," becomes personally efficacious by our faith response – our receptivity of His resurrection-activity.)

Kunneth - (200) - "The new, 'reborn' man is the man who lives from his existential fellowship with the Risen Christ."

Kunneth - (198) - "Being in Christ is an expression for the changed situation which is made possible by the resurrection of Jesus and actualized through the presence of the Risen One. ...the concept of 'being in Christ' is identical with the revealed reality of the resurrection."

Salvation is only through resurrection - I Pet. 3:21. Salvation has been trivialized in evangelical theology: a rescue from the results of sin; fire insurance policy from hell; commodity of eternal life possessed by reason of one's attestation of history and theology; a benefit bestowed by a benefactor. Christians are not only saved "from," but saved "unto" the privileged experience of the r-l of Jesus, the eternal Savior. We are "saved by His life" (Rom. 5:10), as the resurrection-life of Jesus, the "saving life of Christ" is operative in us. Salvation is not escapism, but the restoration of functional humanity.

GRACE

The resurrection-life of the living Lord Jesus can only be lived by the grace of God. Grace is not simply the initiatory action of God to make His Son available to fallen mankind. Grace is God's activation of the Christian life via the grace-expression of the resurrection-life of the living Lord Jesus.The Christian life is the resurrection-life of Jesus, lived only by the enlivening and enabling grace of God. Grace is the divine dynamic which activates the expression of the risen Lord in the Christian.

Jesus was "raised for the purpose of our justification...through whom also we have obtained our introduction by faith into this grace in which we stand" (Rom. 4:25; 5:2)

In the midst of discussing the resurrection, Paul explains that the Risen Lord Jesus appeared to him (I Cor. 15:8) on the road to Damascus, and because of encounter "by the grace of God I am what I am, and His grace toward me did not prove vain; but I labored even more than all of them, yet not I, but the grace of God with me" (I Cor. 15:10). Paul's identity and ministry (cf. Rom. 15:18) are the result of God's grace in the dynamic of the resurrected Jesus.

The grace that energizes the Christian life is always and inevitably the dynamic of the resurrection-life of Jesus Christ.

Moffat (89) - "for Paul the divine power of grace in the resurrection meant everything."

Moffat (91) - "an examination of the theologies of the early church justifies holding that the message of grace was inspired by the resurrection of the Lord Jesus." Grace is a meaningless word apart from the resurrection.

SPIRIT

Since the Holy Spirit is the Spirit of Christ (cf. Rom. 8:9), the work of the Spirit of God is the expression of the resurrection-life of Jesus.

When the Spirit was poured out on Pentecost, Peter explained in the first sermon ever preached in the Church of Jesus Christ, that the promised fulfillment of the Spirit was directly connected to the resurrection of Jesus Christ. The promised Davidic kingdom looked forward to "the resurrection of Christ" (Acts 2:31). "This Jesus God raised up again...having been exalted to the right hand of God, and having received from the Father the promise of the Holy Spirit, He has poured forth this which you both see and hear" (Acts 2:32,33). The work of the Holy Spirit is so inextricably tied to the resurrection reality as to be inseparable.

In the context of attesting to the resurrection, Paul explained that "the first man, Adam, became a living soul. The last Adam became a life-giving Spirit" (I Cor. 15:45). "The Lord is the Spirit" (II Cor. 3:17); the Spirit who gives life (II Cor. 3:6), and that life is the resurrection-life of Jesus. Thus Paul can affirm that "if the Spirit of Him who raised Jesus from the dead dwells in you, He who raised Christ Jesus from the dead will also give life to your mortal bodies through His Spirit who indwells you" (Rom. 8:11).

Kunneth (189) - The actuality of the Risen One cannot be discussed without reference to the Spirit."

Kunneth (190) - "The Spirit is identical with the eternal life of the Risen One."

Kunneth (192) - "indissoluble relationship between the Risen Christ and the Spirit"

Kunneth (193) - "it is only in the resurrection that pneumatology acquires its essential foundation."

Kunneth (193) - "God's Spirit fulfils the original purpose of creation by means of the resurrection of Jesus."

Kunneth (194) - "where the Risen Lord is at work in the present, there the Spirit is working."

Kunneth (194) - "The Christ Spirit means the spiritual reality of the resurrection."

Kunneth (194) - There is no valid pneumatology apart from the resurrection."

DIVINE DYNAMIC / POWER

Tying many of these ideas together, Paul commences his epistle to the Romans by explaining that Jesus was established as the empowering Son of God by His resurrection from the dead, and that in accord with (being the expression of) the Spirit of holiness, Jesus Christ our Lord, through whom we have received grace" (Rom. 1:4). The empowering dynamic of God's grace by the Spirit in the Christian is based upon the historical resurrection event and expressive of the resurrection-life of the risen and living Lord Jesus.

Paul therefore prays that the Ephesian Christians might know "the surpassing greatness of His power...in accordance with the working of the strength of His might which He brought about in Christ, when He raised Him from the dead" (Eph. 1:19,20). It was Paul's personal prayer, as well, as he sought to "know Him, and the power of His resurrection" (Phil. 3:10).

Kunneth (204) - "the ethical dynamic of the Church is a present reality only as the spiritual power of the Risen One." ....results from its existential union with the Risen One."

Kunneth (205) - "the dynamic of the Church is grounded solely in its dependence on the Spirit of the Risen Lord."

Kunneth (205) - "the Church is alive only in so far as it is filled with the power of the resurrection."

CHRISTIAN LIVING

Kunneth - (207) - "Ethical behavior (*living with the character of Christ*) springs from the living reality of the Risen One."

Kunneth (208) - "sanctification...is a reflection of the resurrection within the Church."

Kunneth (209) - "the resurrection has changed the relationship of man to those around him."

LORDSHIP

Acts 2:36 – "Therefore let all the house of Israel know for certain that God has made Him both Lord and Christ—this Jesus whom you crucified."

Kunneth (193) - "it is possible on the ground of the resurrection to speak of the identity of the Lord *Kyrios* with the Spirit." "The Lord is the Spirit" (II Cor. 3:17) can be affirmed as a post-resurrection reality.

CHURCH

Kunneth (195) - "the decisive ground on which the Church became possible is to be seen solely in the resurrection. The impartation of the Spirit associated with Pentecost is obviously dependent on the resurrection."

Kunneth (200) - "the spiritual reality of the Risen Christ begets a new creation, which appears in the spiritual community."

The Kingdom is the resurrection-reign of the risen Lord Jesus.

The historical event of the resurrection must be explained soteriologically and eschatologically, but if we do not go beyond such then we have but an epistemological belief-system based on an historical foundation. Genuine Christianity must proceed to consider the ontological realities of resurrection, the personal encounter and experience that is afforded to the individual who is willing to receive the resurrection-life of Jesus Christ by faith. There is a vast difference between believing the facts of the resurrection-event and assenting to the formulations of the theological explanations of the resurrection, and the ontological reception of the life of the risen Lord Jesus whereby we allow His resurrection-life to be formed in our behavior. One cannot rightfully be considered a Christian unless he has received the living Person of Jesus Christ and is participating in the dynamic expression of His resurrection-life. The ontological reality of resurrection must be received intially and continually in a dynamic continuity of reception.

Resurrection-life is not a logical system – not a data-base to be evaluated. Resurrection is a LIFE to be lived! Jesus Christ living out His life in and through the Christian.

Christianity is not a martyr-religion; not the reverenced idealizing of one who has died for a cause. Its focus is not on a dead person; not on death; not on the cross and crucifixion. It is not a religion of death, but the good news of the vital dynamic of the resurrection-life of Jesus Christ. Much of Western Christianity is preoccupied with death. There is so much emphasis on the cross and on attempts to make mystical experiential applications of death to man's sin - spiritual suppressionism; spiritual flagellation. "Dying to self." Christianity is not a "death-cult" preoccupied with blood and dying.

A careful study of the preaching of the early church in the historical book of the Acts of the Apostles reveals that the clarion call of their message was the resurrection of Jesus Christ.

Acts 1:22 - "a witness with us of His resurrection"

Acts 2:24 - "God raised Him up again, since it was impossible for Him to be held in death's power."

Acts 2:31 - (David) looked ahead and spoke of the resurrection of the Christ."

Acts 2:32 - "This Jesus God raised up again, to which we are all witnesses."

Acts 3:15 - "the one whom God raised from the dead, to which we are all witnesses"

Acts 3:26 - "God raised up His Servant, and sent Him to bless you..."

Acts 4:2 - "they were proclaiming in Jesus the resurrection from the dead"

Acts 4:10 - "Jesus Christ the Nazarene, whom God raised from the dead"

Acts 4:33 - "the apostles were giving witness to the resurrection of the Lord Jesus"

Acts 5:30 - "The God of our Fathers raised up Jesus"

Acts 10:40 - "God raised Him up on the third day, and granted that He should become visible"

Acts 13:30 – "God raised Him from the dead"

Acts 13:33 - "God has fulfilled this promise to our children in that He raised up Jesus"

Acts 13:34 - "He raised Him up from the dead"

Acts 13:37 - "He whom God raised"

Acts 17:3 - "Christ had to suffer and rise again from the dead"

Acts 17:18 - "he was preaching Jesus and the resurrection

Acts 17:31 - "furnished proof to all men by raising Him from the dead"

Acts 26:23 - "by reason of His resurrection from the dead He should be the first to proclaim light both to Jews and to Gentiles"

Christianity is the celebration of the "saving life of Christ" (Rom. 5:10). Life and immortality have been brought to light through the gospel (II Tim. 1:10).

Torrance (*Space Time and Resurrection* - 63) - "When the Protestant doctrine of justification is formulated only in terms of forensic imputation of righteousness or the non-imputation of sins in such a way as to avoid saying that to justify is to make righteous, it is the resurrection that is being by-passed. "We require an active relation to Christ as our righteousness, an active and an actual sharing in His righteousness. This is possible only through the resurrection."

The Extension of the Resurrection

Christians celebrate Easter as the culmination of the Christian year. Why is the remembrance of the resurrection of Jesus Christ the climactic highlight of Christian celebration? Why is the remembrance of Jesus' crucifixion not the ultimate highpoint? Why is the subsequent remembrance of the events of Pentecost not regarded as the culmination of Christian remembrance and worship?

The celebration of Christ's resurrection at Easter by the Christian community focuses Christian worship on the fact that God's ultimate objective for mankind has been achieved in Jesus Christ. What is God's ultimate objective for mankind? Since we were "created for His glory" (Isa. 43:7), and the only way that God can be glorified is when His all-glorious character is manifested within His creation unto His own glory, then the ultimate objective of God for mankind is that His life might be present and operative in mankind, unto His own glory. God's ultimate objective for man is not that man should experience a metaphysical deliverance and be rerouted to a future residence by "going to heaven" someday. Rather, God's objective is that His life might dwell within man and be exhibited through the behavior of mankind, making men fit for earth on the way to heaven.

How, then, is God's ultimate objective for mankind achieved and accomplished in the resurrection of Jesus Christ? The death consequences of man's sin were dealt with in the crucifixion when Jesus vicariously and substitutionally took mankind's sin upon Himself on our behalf. In the redemptive act of His death, Jesus accomplished the remedial work necessary to remedy the consequences of man's sin before God. In that it was "impossible for Him to be held in death's power" (Acts 2:24) for He was personally "without sin" (Heb. 4:15), He was raised from the dead in resurrection. In the resurrection expression of life out of death Jesus accomplished the restorative work of God, allowing the life of God to be restored to man. He took our death in crucifixion that we might have His life by resurrection.

Paul explained in the prologue of his letter to the Romans that God's Son "was declared the Son of God with power by the resurrection from the dead, according to the Spirit of holiness, Jesus Christ our Lord" (Rom. 1:4). Jesus was the eternal Son of God and had displayed the power of God throughout His ministry, but "by the resurrection from the dead" He was declared to have the power to effect the presence and function of God's life in man in order to accomplish God's objective for mankind.

How does the risen Lord Jesus effect this reinvestiture of God's life in man? How is the objective historical resurrection of Jesus Christ made subjectively efficacious in individuals in every century?

Jesus repetitively promised His disciples in the upper room that He would send "another Helper, the Holy Spirit, who would be in them" (cf. Jn. 14:16,17,26,28; 15:26; 16:7,13-17). The word He used for "another" was not *heteros*, meaning "another of a different kind", but He used the word *allos*, meaning "another of the same kind," because He was promising a Helper who would be just like Him since the Helper would be Him in Spirit-form.

Crucified, buried and raised from the dead, Jesus then ascended to the Father (Acts 1:8-11) saying, "you shall receive power when the Holy Spirit has come upon you." Soon thereafter, on Pentecost (Acts 2:14), the Holy Spirit was poured out upon mankind allowing the Spirit of Christ to invest mankind with His life (cf. Acts 2:31-33). "The last Adam (Jesus Christ) became a life-giving Spirit" (I Cor. 15:45). "The Lord (Jesus) who is the Spirit" (II Cor. 3:17) "gives life" (II Cor. 3:6) by His own presence as life in man. God's life, spiritual life, eternal life is in the person of Jesus Christ. Jesus told Martha, "I am the resurrection and the life" (Jn. 11:25), and told His disciples, "I am the way, the truth and the life" (Jn. 14:6). The divine life of God is available to mankind in Jesus Christ. "He that has the Son has life; he that does not have the Son of God does not have life" (I Jn. 5:11,12). When an individual receives the Spirit of Christ into his or her spirit, and "if anyone does not have the Spirit of Christ, he does not belong to Him" (Rom. 8:9), then that person receives Christ as their life (cf. Col. 3:4) and "the Spirit Himself bears witness with our spirit that we are children of God" (Rom. 8:16). The receptivity of His activity of life within us is called "faith." "As many as received Him, to them He gave the right to become children of God, even to those who believe in His name, who were born not of blood, nor of the will of the flesh, nor of the will of man, but of God" (John 1:12,13).

The reinvestiture of God's life in man is accomplished by regeneration. The prerequisite of regeneration is the resurrection of Jesus Christ. Peter explained that we are "born again to a living hope through the resurrection of Jesus Christ from the dead" (I Peter 1:3). In like manner as Jesus experienced life out of death in resurrection, and such rising from the dead was referred to as a "begetting" (Acts 13:33) whereby Jesus was the "first-born from the dead" (Col. 1:18; Rev. 1:5) "among many brethren" (Rom. 8:29), so Christians receive spiritual life out of spiritual death by the receipt of Christ's life in new birth (cf. John 3:1-8). Passing "out of death into life" (John 5:24; I John 3:14), Christians participate in the extension of Christ's resurrection. This is what Paul means by our being "raised up with Him" (Eph. 2:5) and "being made alive together with Christ" (Eph. 2:4). Christians "have been united with Christ in the likeness of His resurrection" (Rom. 6:5) so as to participate in "newness of life" (Rom. 6:4) as a "new creature" (II Cor. 5:17) and a "new man" (Eph. 4:24; Col. 3:10) in Christ Jesus.

If then, as Christians, we "have been raised up with Christ, we are to keep seeking the things above, where Christ is, seated at the right hand of God" (Col. 3:1). But not only is He transcendently "seated at the right hand of God," He is also at the same time immanently present within the spirit of the Christian, "Christ in you the hope of glory" (Col. 1:27). The resurrection-life of Jesus Christ within the spirit of the Christian becomes the empowering of the Christian life. Having promised that "we should receive power when the Holy Spirit had come" (Acts 1:8), Jesus Christ in Spirit-form became that Power of God (I Cor. 1:24) in every Christian. We can "know...the surpassing greatness of His power toward us...which He brought about in Christ, when He raised Him from the dead" (Eph. 1:18-20). In accord with Paul's desire, we can "know the power of His resurrection" (Phil. 3:10) as that "power works within us ... exceedingly abundantly beyond all that we could ask or think" (Eph. 3:20).

We must see beyond the historicity of the empty tomb on that first Easter day, and understand the extension of the resurrection-life and resurrection-power of Jesus Christ in every Christian. Christianity is not just the remembrance of an historical resurrection, but is comprised of the vital dynamic of the risen Lord Jesus functioning in the activity of the Holy Spirit of God by enlivening Christians with the "saving life of Christ" (Rom. 5:10). Christianity is Christ – the resurrected Lord Jesus living out His life in Christians every day, to the glory of God.

RESURRECTION DYNAMIC

Along with Christian communities around the world, we remember the resurrection of Jesus Christ from the dead. It is always a glorious time when Christians gather on Easter to rejoice in the victory of life over death, of Christ over Satan. For almost two millennia the Easter celebration of the resurrection has been the high-point, the culmination of the Christian year.

I want to focus on the on-going import of the resurrection in Christian lives – what I regard to be the essential dynamic of the Christian life – the resurrection-life of the living Lord Jesus.

Let's start with a pop-quiz. If you were asked to pick one of the following categories to indicate what your first and primary thought would be when someone mentioned the resurrection of Jesus Christ, what would you pick?

____ An empty tomb with grave clothes inside

____ Life conquers death

____ The resurrection of our bodies is guaranteed

____ Christ can be our life and live in us

Let me explain that none of these answers is a wrong answer. Each of them is a legitimate perspective and association with the resurrection of Jesus Christ. They are all biblical answers! I think we all like tests like that when there are no wrong answers.

It appears to me that there are three (3) major perspectives by which Christians usually approach their considerations of the resurrection of Jesus Christ. Let's identify those as "the Resurrection Event, the Resurrection Explanation, and the Resurrection Experience."

Within these three approaches to the resurrection of Christ, we can note that the "Resurrection Event" is the "Historical Foundation," of the Christian faith. The "Resurrection Explanation" is the "Theological Formulation" of Christian understanding, whereby the resurrection event is explained. But the "Resurrection Experience" moves beyond the "Historical Foundation" and the "Theological Explanation" to address the "Personal Formation" of the resurrection in the lives of Christian people – the Resurrection Dynamic of Christian life.

Paul wrote to the Galatian Christians. He explains that he "is in labor pains, until Christ is formed in you" (Gal. 4:19). The personal, experiential formation of the resurrection-life of Jesus Christ is essential to the fullness of what the resurrection-dynamic can mean in our Christian lives.

Now, we proceed to the three primary ways that the resurrection of Jesus Christ is usually explained in contemporary Christian teaching. Let's entitle this "The Apologetic Defense of the Resurrection. Focused on the Historical Foundation of the Resurrection Event, and seeking to provide Theological Formulation to explain the Resurrection, Christian teachers and preachers of our day often utilize the resurrection narrative to attempt to defend the historicity of Jesus – that He **really was** born, and lived, and died on the cross, and rose from the dead on the third day. Frank Morison wrote a book years ago entitled *Who Moved the Stone*, wherein he employed his legal arguments as a lawyer to verify and justify the historicity of the Resurrection Event. Josh McDowell published a book on *Resurrection* that employed similar techniques of apologetics to attempt to prove the historicity of the resurrection event. In a world of people increasingly skeptical of the historical and factual data of Jesus' life on earth, such apologetic arguments seldom convince many of the historical veracity of Jesus, much less to receive Jesus as Savior and Lord of their lives.

Many other preachers and teachers use Easter morning and the Resurrection Event of Jesus' resurrection to attempt to defend the Deity of Jesus in the ultimate divine miracle of Jesus being raised from the dead. Attempting to prove and defend the deity of Jesus by means the resurrection miracle seldom convinces many skeptics.

We often observe Christian teachers and preachers using the Resurrection Event to give a Resurrection Explanation that defends the expectation of the bodily resurrection of Christians in the future. This is not an invalid argument, for Paul uses this argument in I Corinthians 15 to explain that "if Christ be not raised from dead, our faith is in vain," for if Christ is raised from the dead it serves as the guarantee that we, too, as Christians, shall experience bodily resurrection from the dead in the future determinations of God.

I think many people, including Christian people in the pews of the churches across America, are wanting to know WHY Christ was raised from the dead in an explanation that relates to how they live their lives day-by-day.

The Resurrection of Jesus is central and primary to our identity as a people and as a church fellowship. We are obliged to be able to share with people the FULL implications of WHY Jesus was raised from the dead on that first Easter morning.

So, what I am suggesting and emphasizing this morning is that a complete "Apologetic defense of the Resurrection of the Son of God needs to include "a defense of the reality of the risen Lord Jesus living in us." We do not want to think of the resurrection merely as a past historical event that we can explain theologically. Now do we want to project the implications of the resurrection of Jesus Christ only to a future realization when our bodies will be raised after death. It is of supreme importance that we explain to people that the resurrection is the dynamic of our personal Christian experience in the present as we allow the resurrection-life of the risen and living Lord Jesus to live in us and be our life.

When the report came to Jesus that His friend, Lazarus, had died, Jesus came to Bethany, and said to Martha, "I AM the resurrection and the Life."

resurrected, risen Son of God, the living Lord Jesus, is the very first word of our identification. We should ... we must ... be characterized by the Resurrection Dynamic of the Risen Son.

The risen Lord Jesus, ...ALIVE, ...dwelling in us, ... raised to "newness of life" in us, ... functioning as our life ... must be represented (not just represented, but re-presented in our daily lives and behavior). The community around us should be able to detect that we Christians have something unique about their lives and character. They may not be able to put their finger on it, but the resurrection-dynamic of the risen and living Lord Jesus will be manifested in our mortal bodies (II Cor. 4:10).

Is that something that we can "pull off," self-generate, and produce? NO!

Religious self-effort will never be able to convince people that they are seeing the risen Son of God living His life out in us. NEVER. The resurrection-dynamic of the living Lord Jesus can only be effected by the power of God, the GRACE of God – Jesus alive in us!

In Phil. 3:10, Paul prayed that he might know "the power of His resurrection." The Greek word for the "power" of His resurrection is *dunamis*, the word from which we get "dynamite," and the word from which we get "resurrection-**dynamic.**" This is always, and only, a God-thing – the supernatural power of God's GRACE exhibiting the Christ-life, the resurrection-life of Jesus in our lives.

If we are willing to use "Easter" as a verb, we can say that the risen Lord Jesus is "EASTERING" in us – day by day, moment by moment, in our relationship with our spouses, when we are interacting with colleagues or co-workers, when we are parenting, in every facet of our daily lives. "It is no longer I who lives, but Christ lives in me" (Gal. 2:20). "Christ in me, the hope of glory" (Col. 1:27) – the expectation of glorifying God in the living Lord Jesus by the power/dynamic of His Holy Spirit.

May this be true, an evident reality, in the Christians, the Christ-ones, who fellowship and commune in our fellowship.

The Living Reality of the Resurrection

I observed a sign outside of a local church building. That seems to be the "in-thing" in ecclesiastical circles these days – to post trite sayings on a display sign so the world can observe their superficiality (or stupidity). This sign read, "The CROSS – That's My (God's) final answer."

What do you think of that statement?

As a take-off from the contemporary television program, "Who Wants to be a Millionaire," where each contestant must verify, "That's my final answer," I found the statement cute and catchy. Theologically, I found the statement inaccurate and misleading.

If the cross is God's final answer, then what are we doing here today? Is Easter an irrelevancy?

If the death of Jesus on the execution instrument of a cross is the final answer, then Jesus is just a martyr figure that Christians rally around to persuade others to join their cause – in this case, their religion.

Martin Luther King is such a martyr figure for the blacks in America, allowing them to emphasize their cause of victimization in the history and policies of America.

Che Guevera is such a martyr figure for some Hispanics, serving as a focal point to emphasize their oppression at the hands of others.

Sayyid Qutb is such a martyr figure for the Muslims, serving as a springboard for radical Islamic terrorism to combat Western civilization. Maybe Saddam Hussein will become a martyr figure for some Arabs in the years to come.

But is that all that Jesus is for Christians?

If the cross is an end in itself, i.e. "God's final answer," then all the gruesome execution of Jesus can do is create a martyr figure that allows people to focus on the death of this individual in order to perpetuate a particular ideology. Granted, that is how much of the Christian religion operates in our day, but is that what Christianity was intended to be?

What happened on the cross, the death of Jesus, represents a remedial action. A remedial action is action taken to remedy a problem of deficiency. Many students, for example, are required to take remedial math or remedial English courses in order to qualify for college level courses. The remedial courses remedy and correct the problem of these students' deficient understanding of the subjects. The problem that needed to be remedied for the human race was a deficiency that disqualified mankind from being man as God intended, and thus from participating in the course of life as God intended man to live.

Original man (represented by Adam and Eve) was given the choice of life and death in the garden. The life choice was to receive from the "tree of life" which represented the derivation of God's life operative in man. The death choice was to partake of the "tree of the knowledge of good and evil," concerning which God had said, "In the day that you eat thereof, you will surely die" (Gal. 2:17). Was that a threat by a God who would take punitive action if His intents were violated? Or was that simply a statement of inevitable fact, indicating that the rejection of the power of God's life would be to open themselves up to the only alternative of "the one having the power of death, that is the devil" (Heb. 2:14) functioning in them?

The original sin of the original couple (who represented all humanity) allowed death to reign (Rom. 5:17) in the human race. The resultant deficiency of divine life in mankind (fallen man is "devoid of the Spirit" - Jude 19) disqualified humanity from being man as God intended. That is why remedial action was necessitated - so that man could enroll again in the course of life!

The Son of God, who was incarnated as the man, Jesus, was willing to enroll in the remedial course of death on man's behalf - as an alternative representative man for humanity. He was willing to submit to death, though personally undeserving of such for He was "without sin" (Heb. 4:12; II Cor. 5:21), so that representatively He might substitutionally assume the death consequences of mankind's sin, and allow His divine life to overcome the "power of death" and make His life available to humanity again.

It makes a difference how we interpret the death of Jesus. Was God the Father an offended deity demanding that a penalty of death be paid for sin before He would forgive mankind? A popular view of the crucifixion seems to cast God as an angry, bloodthirsty, death-dealing God who poured out His punitive wrath and judgment upon His Son, Jesus, because "somebody's gotta pay!" Jesus, the Son of God, is often portrayed, on the other hand, as a loving and forgiving side of God who was willing to express divine grace in order to redeem man instead of demanding justice and judgment. What does such a perspective do to God? It divides and divorces the intents of the Father and the Son. It severs the Trinity asunder. The Father is *against* us; the Son is *for* us. The Son is acting as our legal advocate attempting to convince the

Father, the Judge, to let us off the hook. What a tragic mangling of the oneness of the Triune God.

On the contrary, the Father, Son and Holy Spirit had a unified intent to restore humanity to the divine intent. God was wholly *for* us in His divine love and grace, and was desirous that death, and "the one having the power of death" (Heb. 2:14) be defeated by assuming death undeservedly via the Son's assumption of mortal humanity. The restoration of God's life *to* man required the assumption of death *for* man. God's affirmative "*Yes*" to man's redemption and restoration, required the "*No*" to the death invasion of sin. Via the crucifixion of Jesus on the cross, God said "*No*" to the misuse and abuse of humanity by the diabolic death-dealing antithesis to the living God, "the god of this age" (II Cor. 4:4). God would no longer tolerate the "one having the power of death" (Heb. 2:14) to hold man hostage (II Tim. 1:14).

The death of Jesus on the cross was the undoing of the Adamic downfall as Jesus voluntarily accepted the death consequences of humanity's sin. "Obedient unto death, even death on a cross" (Phil. 2:8), Jesus was "made sin" (II Cor. 5:21) on our behalf. He was personally sinless, however, and "it was impossible for Him to be held in death's power" (Acts 2:24), by the usurping death-agent, "the one having the power of death, that is the devil" (Heb. 2:14).

From the cross, Jesus exclaimed, "*Tetelestai* – It is Finished!" He knew that in the death He was dying, He would "accomplish what the Father had sent Him to do" (Jn. 17:4) as a mortal man. He knew that He would "finish" the death captivation of man by the death-dealing destroyer (I Cor. 10:10) of man. He knew that His assumption of death would inevitably allow for the rising forth of divine resurrection life made available to all men for their restoration.

The resurrection of Jesus from the dead was God's "*Yes*" to the restoration of His divine life in humanity. If our theology does not go beyond redemption in the death of Jesus on the cross, to the restoration of God's life in humanity by the resurrection, then it ceases to be Christian theology. God's "final answer" was not the cross. God's final answer was (and is) the resurrection! In the resurrection of Jesus divine life overcame death, God overcame Satan (I Jn. 3:8; Heb. 2:14). That was historically enacted on that third day when Jesus arose from the dead and exited the tomb, but it was for the purpose of resurrection being personally and spiritually enacted in those receptive to Christ by faith.

It is a sad indictment of contemporary Christian religion to observe how the resurrection is regarded and taught in the churches today. It has become but a token recollection in the annual church calendar.

There will be many sermons in the pulpits of the churches across the world today that adduce a list of apologetic arguments as proofs that the resurrection of Jesus really took place as the gospel writers record. They will be attempting to prove that the physical resurrection of Jesus was indeed an *historical miracle* that attests to the supernatural power and ability of God. They will be building scaffolding around the doctrine of the historical resurrection of Jesus, apparently concerned that this tenet of their faith might crumble and fall if they cannot convince people that God is capable of accomplishing such an historical miracle, and that it really did occur as an historical event. When the primary objective of popular preaching is to attest to the possibility and accuracy of the historical miracle of Jesus' resurrection, it tends to have a boomerang effect on the preaching of the gospel. If the historical resurrection needs to be propped up with all this scaffolding of support as the preachers engage in apologetic defensiveness, then what kind of an impotent God do they believe in? If we believe in a sovereign and omnipotent God, then we can accept the miracle of the resurrection as an historical "given."

Many other Easter messages will be approaching the resurrection of Jesus as a *theological argument* to verify and prove the deity of Jesus Christ. They seek to explain that the historical miracle of the resurrection lends credence to the Christian claim that Jesus was really God in the flesh. Why do Christians spend so much time and energy trying to apologetically defend the basic tenets of their faith? If God is a God of miracles, as He is, and Jesus is the divine Son of God, as He is, then why don't Christians begin to build a practicum of application that pertains to the practical ramifications of Christ's resurrection in contemporary life? If it doesn't apply to our daily lives, then Christianity is just an historical society for the remembrance of the events of Jesus' life, or a theological society to contend about the varied explanations of His life. Let's get on with life!

Still avoiding the present implications of resurrection life, another theological argument based on the resurrection of Jesus is to use the historical miracle of the resurrection as verification for the expectation of the future resurrection of Christians after death. This was, of course, Paul's argument in that great "resurrection chapter" of I Corinthians 15, but a more comprehensive study reveals that the over-all emphasis on resurrection in Paul's epistles is not just to connect the past resurrection of Jesus in history to the future resurrection of bodies in heaven. Paul's primary concern was to demonstrate how the historical resurrection of Jesus served as the triumphant presentation of life out of death, the victory of divine life over diabolic death.

The need of the hour in Christian preaching and teaching is to proclaim the resurrection as a *living reality* wherein the living Lord Jesus is presently indwelling Christians and living out His resurrection life in Christian behavior. Though Christianity has historical foundations and theological explanations, the vital dynamic that validates Christianity is that Jesus Christ is alive today by the Spirit to indwell the spirits of receptive individuals who will allow Him to live out His life and character in their behavior.

In declaring the purpose of His coming, Jesus said, "I came to give My life a ransom for many" (Matt. 20:28; Mk. 10:45). He came to die and to allow His death to take the death consequences for all men, releasing them from the grasp of the death-dealing devil. He also said, "I came that you might have life, and have it more abundantly" (Jn. 10:10). He knew that His death would result in resurrection, life out of death, for the sin-source and death-dealer would not be able to capture Him, the Sinless One. His resurrection would allow God's life to become operative in mankind again as each individual with freedom of choice was willing to receive such life.

The power to bestow and restore God's life to sinful and fallen mankind was given to Jesus upon His resurrection. Paul explains, "He was declared the Son of God with power (the power to convey life out of death) by the resurrection from the dead" (Rom. 1:4). "Christ is the power of God" (I Cor. 1:24) for the re-lifing, the spiritual regeneration of humanity.

In that great resurrection chapter of I Corinthians 15, Paul wrote, "The first man, Adam, became a living soul. The last Adam (Jesus) became a life-giving spirit" (I Cor. 15:45). The first representative man, Adam, became a living soul when God breathed into him the breath of lives (Gen. 2:7), the spiritual life of Father, Son and Holy by which he could have functioned as God intended by deriving God's life. But he made the death choice rather than the life choice. Jesus, on the other hand, is the other representative man who came to restore God's life to man. He is called the "Last Adam," the *Eschatos* Man, the last in a sequence of two alternatives. Earlier in the same chapter, Paul wrote, "As in Adam all die, so also in Christ all shall be made alive" (I Cor. 15:22). All men are united representatively and spiritually with either Adam or Christ, in either spiritual death or spiritual life. The "last Adam," Jesus Christ, who came as God-man to die on our behalf, became (by His resurrection and ascension and Pentecostal outpouring) the "life-giving Spirit" to give God's life to the spirits of receptive persons. To the Corinthians, Paul wrote, "Now the Lord (Jesus) is the Spirit" (II Cor. 3:17), and "the Spirit gives life" (II Cor. 3:6). The risen and living Lord Jesus now functions as the "Spirit of Christ" (Rom. 8:9) restoring spiritual life to those seeking, desiring, and willing to receive it.

This spiritual life that the Spirit of Christ makes available to mankind is not a detached package of "eternal life" that is but a "benefit" of believing in Jesus. The life that the living Lord Jesus makes available to mankind is Himself. "I AM the resurrection and the life" (Rom. 11:25), Jesus said to Martha, identifying Himself with the I AM of God (Exod. 3:14). "I AM the way, the truth, and the life" (Jn. 14:6), Jesus explained to His disciples. Jesus is the modality (way), the reality (truth), and the vitality (life) of God Himself. The need of fallen mankind is the restoration of the presence of God's life in their spirit to energize their behavior in soul and body. The Spirit of Christ is that life. Life is a Person. "I AM the life" (Jn. 14:6), Jesus said. Divine life, spiritual life, eternal life, resurrection life are all the life of the risen and living Lord Jesus. The Apostle John explained, "He that has the Son has the life; he who does not have the Son of God does not have the life" (I Jn. 5:12).

How does man partake of the life that is the resurrected Jesus? The apostle Peter indicated that we are "born again to a living hope through the resurrection of Jesus

Christ from the dead" (I Pet. 1:3). The resurrection of Jesus was the prerequisite to the restoration of divine life in man. Using the metaphor of birth for the initiation of life, Jesus told Nicodemus, "You must be born again" (Jn. 3:7). "Unless one is born from above" (Jn. 3:3), receiving the spiritual life that is God's life, an individual will not be restored to God's intent, for God so designed man that it requires the presence of God's life in man for man to be man as God intended man to be. While still speaking to Nicodemus, Jesus made that most familiar statement, "God so loved the world that He gave His only begotten Son, that whoever *believes* in Him should not perish, but have eternal life" (Jn. 3:16). To believe is more than just mental assent or affirmation to historical or theological data. To *believe* is to *receive*. John wrote, "As many as *received* Him, to them He gave the right to become children of God, even to those who *believe* in His name, who were born not of blood, nor of the will of the flesh, nor of the will of man, but of God" (Jn. 1:12,13). There are no proprietary procedures for an individual's reception of the life that is Jesus. It doesn't have to happen in a church by walking an aisle, or raising one's hand, or repeating a "statement of faith." It doesn't have to happen by consenting to "four spiritual laws" and praying a "prayer of faith." An individual simply has to get real with God and desire the life that only God can give.

Jesus said, "Truly, truly, I say to you, he who hears My word, and believes Him who sent Me, has eternal life, and does not come into judgment, but has passed out of death into life" (Jn. 5:24). The one who believes and receives the Spirit of Christ has "passed out of death into life" (I Jn. 3:14). When one becomes a Christian in this way, he participates in a spiritual re-enactment of the death and resurrection of Jesus. To the Roman Christians, Paul explained, "Do you not know that all who have been baptized into Christ Jesus have been baptized into His death?" (Rom. 6:3). "For if we have become united with

Him in the likeness of His death, certainly we shall be also in the likeness of His resurrection" (Rom. 6:5), "in order that as Christ was raised from the dead through the glory of the Father, so we too might walk in newness of life" (Rom. 6:4). "Now if we have died with Christ, we believe that we shall also live with Him" (Rom. 6:8). "So consider yourselves to be dead to sin, but alive to God in Christ Jesus" (Rom. 6:11). The person that we were, the "old man," "has been crucified with Christ" (Rom. 6:6) and "laid aside" (Eph. 4:22; Col. 3:9), and the Christian is now a "new man" (Eph. 4:24; Col. 3:10), a "new creature" in Christ (II Cor. 5:17), "raised up with Christ" (Col. 3:1), raised up to newness of life by His resurrection life. To the Colossians, Paul wrote, "You were raised up with Him through faith in the working of God, who raised Him from the dead... He made you alive together with Him" (Col. 2:12,13). The divine life that we receive as Christians is His resurrection life. "Christ is our life" (Col. 3:4).

The Christian life is the Christ life dwelling within us and operating through us. "Christ lives in me," Paul exclaimed, "and the life that I now live I live by faith in the Son of God who loved me and gave Himself up for me" (Gal. 2:20). "Do you not recognize this about yourselves, that Jesus Christ is in you?" (II Cor. 13:5), Paul asked the Corinthian Christians. "For me, to live is Christ" (Phil. 1:21), Paul explained to the Philippians. The power of God that raised Jesus from the dead is the living power that is now working in us (Eph. 1:18-21), Paul revealed in his prayer for the Christians of Ephesus. Christianity is Christ – living His resurrection life in us.

If the only explanation for me, and the life that I live, is not the living Lord Jesus, then I'm not being Christian. If I'm not different because Jesus is alive in me and living through me (not weird-different or sensational-different, but character-different), then what good is all this resurrection-talk? If the resurrection life of the Spirit of

Christ is not lived out in us, validating the *living reality* of the resurrection, then let the Christian historians dabble with their archaeological data; let the Christian theologians argue about their religious explanations; let the Christian preachers and their parishioners "play church;" for it is all an exercise in futility. If the resurrection doesn't become *living reality* in our lives, Sunday, Monday, Tuesday, Wednesday, Thursday, Friday, and Saturday of every week of every year, then Jesus died and rose again in vain – just "for the fun of it." God forbid!

Christianity is not just another ideological option that one can stack up against other ideas, and by human reasoning "take it or leave it." Christianity is not an epistemological belief-system – a "believe-right" religion. Christianity is not a morality system of right and wrong – a "do-right" religion. Christianity is Christ. Christ is life. The option that human creatures have because of Jesus Christ is life or death. Divine life is available in Him, but the choice is ours. As choosing creatures, we can passively choose by our non-choice (i.e. rejection) of Jesus to participate in the only other alternative, the present and everlasting consequences of death. Remember, God is not the punitive, death-dealing God that has determined to judge people and send them to hell. God doesn't send anyone to hell, but He does respect mankind enough as the choosing creature that He created him to be, to allow an individual to choose the perpetuity of identification with "the one having the power of death, that is the devil" (Heb. 2:14). "God is not willing that any should perish, but that all might come to repentance" (II Pet. 3:9) and life in Christ Jesus.

A CALL FOR RESURRECTION THEOLOGY

The church throughout the centuries has often failed to recognize the significance of the resurrection of Jesus. Despite the fact that the Easter celebration has been regarded as the culmination of the Christian year of worship, the full meaning of the resurrection has often been undeveloped or diluted in Christian teaching and preaching. Christian theology has emphasized numerous legitimate Biblical themes, but has seldom made the resurrection the focal point or fulcrum on which all other Christian subjects depend. Roman Catholic theologian, Claude Geffré, laments,

> "As strange as it may seem, the resurrection of Christ, which sums up all of Christianity, has still not been the object of any exhaustive reflection within dogmatic theology. The remark has often been made that the theology manuals devote little space to the resurrection compared to the long elaborations dealing with the divinity of Christ or with his redeeming mission. And even today, rare are the theologians who choose the resurrection of Christ as the organizing principle of Christology." [1]

Because of this neglect and the common misemphases of Christian theology, I am compelled to write this article and to make "a call for resurrection theology."

Historical emphases of Christian religion

As we evaluate Christian thought through the centuries, we note that different segments of the church have tended to emphasize different historical events in the life of Jesus. The two primary events thus emphasized are the *birth* of Jesus and the *death* of Jesus.

Roman Catholic theology has tended to emphasize the birth of Jesus in the theology of the incarnation. Emphasis is placed on Mary, the birth mother of Jesus, and upon the virgin birth of Jesus. This is not to say that Roman Catholic theology has neglected the death of Jesus in crucifixion, as is obviated by the crucifix symbol that is found in all Catholic churches and in many Catholic homes, but the primary emphasis to explain Jesus as the God-man has seemingly been on the incarnational birth of Jesus.

Protestant theology, on the other hand, has for almost five hundred years tended to emphasize the death of Jesus in crucifixion, focusing on the cross and the sacrificial blood of Jesus. The Reformation emphasis was on the substitutionary sacrifice of Christ as an expiatory action that propitiated God's judgment on man and reconciles sinners to God so that they may be declared justified.

Australian author, Robert D. Brinsmead, comments, "It is well known that Catholicism made the Incarnation central to its theology, while Protestantism made the atonement of the cross the central thing."[2] The Scottish preacher and New Testament scholar, James S. Stewart, wrote similarly, "Protestant theology, concentrating on the atoning sacrifice of the cross, has not always done justice to the apostolic emphasis on the risen life."[3]

Stewart followed up by noting that, "Protestant theology, in some of its phases, has unconsciously altered the apostolic accent by almost isolating the cross, and failing to see Calvary with the Resurrection light breaking behind it."[4]

It is important to understand that the objective, historical events of incarnation and crucifixion, the birth and the death of the historical, physical Christ were remedial measures enacted by God to remedy the problem of man's sin; to provide the solution to the fall of humanity into sin in Adam.

If the incarnation and crucifixion were the only historical acts of God on man's behalf, then the gospel would cease to be "good news". If the gospel narrative was only that "Jesus was born. Jesus died. God said to man: 'There is the remedy! I came. I fixed the problem. Now you are fixed. The slate is wiped clean. Now, go and do a better job next time.'" That is not good news! That is damnable doctrine. That is tragic teaching!

The incarnation and crucifixion alone serve only to condemn man all the more. The story would go like this: "A man came who was God-man. He did not share the spiritual depravity of the rest of mankind. He did not develop the "flesh" patterning of selfish desires like other men. He lived life as God intended, allowing God in him to manifest His desire and character at every moment in time for thirty-three years. He was the perfect man! He did not deserve to die, but He was put to death unjustly. In dying undeservedly, He died in our place, as our substitute, and paid the price of death to satisfy God's justice, and forgive mankind of their sins." Is that the whole of the story? If so, He lived and died perfectly which we cannot do. If the incarnation and crucifixion were the whole of the story, then we would have been better off without Him! Why? Because *He could* live and die as He did; *we cannot*. And the fact that *He did* only condemns us all the more by His matchless example, for *we do not* have what it takes to live like that.

Only in the resurrection do we have the message that God has given us the provision of His life in order that we might be man as God intended man to be; in order that the resurrection life of the risen Lord Jesus might become the essence of spiritual life in the Christian; in order that we might live by His life and the expression of His character. The resurrection is the positive provision of life in Christ Jesus, around which all other theological topics must be oriented.

As Walter Kunneth concludes,

> "The raising of the Christ is ***the*** act of God, whose significance is not to be compared with any event before or after. It is the *primal datum of theology*, from which there can be no abstracting, and the normative presupposition for every valid dogmatic judgment and for the meaningful construction of a Christian theology. Thus, the resurrection of Jesus becomes the Archimedean point for theology. All theological statements are oriented in one way or another toward this focal point. There is no Christian knowledge of God which does not acquire its ultimate fullness and depth from a revelation of God in the Risen One." [5]

Christian theology, in both its Catholic and Protestant forms, has failed to recognize the resurrection as the central feature of its theology, and has often thereby abdicated and defaulted in explaining the significance of the resurrection of Jesus.

Emphases of resurrection in Christian religion

When Christian religion has attempted to address the resurrection in its theological considerations, it has done so in a way that continues to short-change the significance of the resurrection. The resurrection in Christian theology has been relegated to apologetic arguments of historicity, defence of Jesus' deity, and futuristic expectations of bodily resurrection.

Christian religion has emphasized the historicity of the resurrection of Jesus, employing a variety of sources to document, authenticate, and validate the historical resurrection of Jesus. Apologists like Frank Morison (*Who Moved the Stone?*[6]) and Josh McDowell (*The Resurrection Factor* [7]) have sought to provide Christians with historical "proofs" for the resurrection of Jesus.

Having "proven" the historical veracity of the resurrection by their chronological and logical evidences, Christian religion has then emphasized that the resurrection of Jesus was a supernatural miracle that verifies the divinity or deity of Jesus. The resurrection of Jesus has been used as a tool for apologetic defence, as a leverage to authorize and "prove" Christ's divinity and the church's teaching.

As Robert D. Brinsmead explains, "The so-called 'historical proofs' of the resurrection have been marshalled, not to explore the meaning of the mystery itself, but to validate the church's claims about the divinity of Jesus, the authority of the church, and its possession of an exclusive and absolute truth."[8] Claude Geffré likewise comments that,

> "since the end of the nineteenth century the resurrection of Christ has become the favorite object of Christian apologetics. It was a matter of establishing the historicity of the resurrection in order to furnish a proof for the divinity of Christ and thereby accredit his message and its legitimacy. And when apologetics had defended the historical character of the *miracle* of the resurrection, it seemed dogmatic theology had no more to say about the *mystery* of the resurrection." [9]

On the basis of the historicity of Jesus' resurrection and the theological establishment of His deity, Christian religion has proceeded to emphasize that the primary theological import of the historical resurrection of Jesus is to validate the assurance of the eventual resurrection of Christians' bodies in the future. The historical, physical resurrection of Jesus is used as the foundational basis for authenticating the expected bodily resurrection of the Christian after death.

Is this not the argument that Paul uses in I Corinthians 15 in the "Resurrection chapter"? Yes it is, but this is not the entirety of what Paul had to say about the subject of resurrection. Though it is the most extended passage that he seems to have written on the subject, it is not the predominant or primary emphasis that Paul makes concerning the resurrection. The historical *sitz im leben* context of I Corinthians was that the Corinthians were so enamored with their present "spirituality" that they were eschewing or denying anything beyond the present. To counter this triumphalistic diminishment of hope, and to correct Hellenic concepts that deprecated embodiment, Paul ties the bodily resurrection of Jesus with the expected bodily resurrection of Christians.

In so doing, Paul does not necessarily imply that the resurrected physical body of Jesus is prototypical of the resurrected body of the Christian after death. The physicality of the resurrected body is not the issue Paul was addressing.

Secondly, it must be noted that the predominance of Paul's references to the resurrection of Jesus do not relate to the future bodily resurrection of Christians. Paul's primary inference from the resurrection of Jesus is that anyone who is receptive in faith to the living Lord Jesus can be spiritually raised to newness of life (cf. Rom. 6:4,5) by the resurrection life of the living Jesus. Paul emphasized the present availability of life in Christ, and avoided lapsing back into the Jewish framework of theology that he had espoused in the past.

Jewish theology was always a theology of future expectation. As can be noted throughout the Old Testament (the old covenant literature), the Jewish people were always looking for fulfilment in the future; the prophetic promise of that which was yet to come. Regrettably, Christian theology has often fallen prey to just such future expectations in a reversion to a Jewish paradigm of theological expectations.

New covenant Christian theology, as expressed in the New Testament, emphasizes that God's promises and man's expectations are realized in Jesus Christ. Christian theology looks back to the "finished work" of Jesus Christ (cf. John 17:4; 19:30). Christians are "complete in Christ" (Col. 3:10). Christian theology is a realized theology (cf. I Cor. 3:21-23; II Pet. 1:3). The emphasis is not on "it is coming," but on "it is done!" for the whole of God's intent is in the risen and living Lord Jesus.

The emphases of Christian religion on resurrection have traditionally been on proving the historical accuracy of Jesus' resurrection in order to authenticate His divinity, which in turn has been used to convince and assure Christians of an eventual bodily resurrection after physical death.

If Christian theology does not get beyond the cradle and the cross, the birth and the death of Jesus, then all we have to offer is a static history lesson with no contemporary consequence. If Christian theology does not get beyond apologetic defence for what "was", and longing expectation for what "will be," then it becomes an irrelevancy of temporalized "bookends" that fails to address what "is" and "should be" presently.

H.A. Williams explains that,

> "Resurrection, at least in Western Christendom, has invariably been described as belonging to another time and place. The typical emphasis has been upon the past and future – a past and future with which our connection can only be theoretical... So, for example, a book about the resurrection is naturally assumed to be a discussion either about what can be held to have happened in the environs of Jerusalem and Galilee on the third day after Jesus was crucified or about what can be held to be in store for us after our own death.
>
> When resurrection is considered in terms of past and future, it is robbed of its impact on the present. That is why for most of the time resurrection means little to us. It is remote and isolated."
>
> It is a neat trick...this banishing of resurrection to past and future. It saves us from a lot of reality and delivers us from a great deal of fear. It has, in short, the advantage of safeguarding us from life." [10]

What a tragedy that the Christian religion has itself blockaded people from life in Christ by projecting the implications of the resurrection to an historical event of the past or to an anticipated expectation of the future. These are not the predominant emphases of resurrection in the new covenant literature of the New Testament as we shall proceed to note.

Present Dynamic of Life emphasis in Resurrection Theology

This is a call for a Resurrection Theology that emphasizes the present dynamic of life in the risen and living Lord Jesus. Such Resurrection theology will be a restoration of Biblical theology as previewed in the literature of the Old Testament and explained by the New Testament writers.

Everything in the old covenant (Old Testament) was but a pictorial prefiguring of what God was going to do in the resurrection of His Son, Jesus.

The resurrection was a replay of the Genesis account of "coming into being", for the resurrection of the "last Adam" (I Cor. 15:45) allows for God's breathing "the spirit of life" (cf. Gen. 2:7) into man again that he might once again become a spiritually alive soul. Mankind is re-genesised in spiritual regeneration, becoming a "new creature" (II Cor. 5:17) as part of a "new creation" (Gal. 6:15).

Resurrection is likewise the basis for the spiritual reportrayal of the Exodus story, bringing mankind out of the land of slavery into the promised land. Christ's coming out of the grave can be seen to correspond to Moses and his people coming out of Egypt, wherein the resurrection becomes the liberating exodus of salvation history.

It is by the resurrection that we have the spiritual restructuring of the *Torah* as detailed in Exodus, Leviticus, Numbers and Deuteronomy. The external codification of Law becomes an internal dynamic of "the law written in our hearts" (Jere. 31:33; Heb. 8:10; 10:16). Christ becomes "the end of the Law" (Rom. 10:4) as its completion and fulfilment, for the living Lord Jesus expresses the character of God in man as the Law required. The behavioral performance commitments of "we will do it" (Exod. 19:8; 24:3,7), are transformed by the dynamic provision of Christ's resurrection life whereby "He will bring it to pass" (I Thess. 5:24).

The history of Israel becomes His-story as the resurrected Jesus establishes the Davidic Kingdom (Acts 13:34) of divine intent. Those in Christ become the "chosen race", the "people of God" (I Peter 2:9,10), the spiritual Israel of God (Gal. 6:16; Rom. 9:6).

The resurrection is a transformation of the psalms and songs of God, as those participating in the resurrection sing a "new song", singing "spiritual songs in their hearts to God" (Eph. 5:19; Col. 3:16).

All of the prophetic promises of God for His people are affirmed by the "Yes" and "Amen" (II Cor. 1:20) of God's completed action in the resurrection of His Son, Jesus Christ.

The entire Old Testament, (old covenant) was but a preliminary blueprint that pictorially pointed to the resurrection of Jesus. The resurrection of Christ wraps up the physical prefiguring of the old covenant, and is the culminating and continuing action of God that makes all things new in the eternal new covenant.

The new covenant (New Testament) literature is obviously more directly focused on the resurrection of Jesus Christ, for the resurrection is the dynamic reality that is the essence of the new covenant.

All four gospel narratives (Matthew, Mark, Luke and John) culminate and climax with the account of Jesus' resurrection from the dead. But even prior to the historical enactment of His physical resurrection, Jesus had revealed that His resurrection would have an extended and eternal impact. He declared to Martha, "I AM the resurrection and the life" (John 11:25). To the Jews in the temple, Jesus foretold that the temple of His body would be destroyed, but raised in three days" (John 6:19-22), indicating that by His resurrection the new center of worship would be in Him. Later He told the Jews that He would "raise men up in the last day" (John 6:39-44), the finalization of the new covenant.

Luke's account of the progressive advance of the early church in *The Acts of the Apostles* reveals that the *kerygma*, the preached message, of the apostles was centered in the resurrection of Jesus. Peter declares in the first sermon of the church that "God raised Him up, ...because it was impossible for Him to be held in death's power" (Acts 2:24), and "this Jesus God raised up, to which we are all witnesses" (Acts 2:32). In Peter's second sermon he proclaimed, "God raised up His Servant and sent Him to bless you by turning everyone from your wicked ways" (Acts 3:26, cf.15). The resurrection was the message, the theology, of the early church (cf. Acts 4:10,33; 5:30; 10:40; 13:30,34), as they were "preaching Jesus and the resurrection" (Acts 17:18).

The Apostle Paul, having met the risen Lord Jesus on the road to Damascus (Acts 9:3-8; 22:6-11; 26:12-19), had no concept of a gospel apart from the dynamic implications of the resurrected Jesus who had become his life (Gal. 2:20; Phil. 1:21; Col. 3:4). In his brief recitation of the foundational historical events of the gospel, Paul explains that "Christ *died* for our sins, ...was *buried*, ...and was *raised* on the third day" (I Cor. 15:1-4), but whereas the verbs "died" and "buried" were Greek aorist tenses of the past, his verb choice for Jesus "having been raised" was the Greek perfect tense that conveys a past event with present consequences. The resurrection of Jesus was never mere history in the thinking of Paul; it was always the present dynamic life and power of the risen Lord within him.

To the Romans Paul noted that Jesus was "declared the Son of God with power by the resurrection from the dead," being now "the Spirit of holiness, Jesus Christ our Lord" (Rom. 1:4). Jesus became, by His resurrection, the "life-giving Spirit" (I Cor. 15:45), the "Spirit of life" (Rom. 8:2), the "Spirit of Christ" (Rom. 8:9) who invests His resurrection life in those individuals receptive to such by faith, and without which "they are none of His" (Rom. 8:9). "The Spirit of Him who raised Jesus from the dead dwells in you," Paul asserts, and "He who raised Jesus from the dead will give life to your mortal bodies through His Spirit who indwells you" (Rom. 8:11).

Paul wanted Christians to understand that they had been subjectively and spiritually "united with Christ in His resurrection" (Rom. 6:5) and "raised to walk in newness of life" (Rom. 6:4) in the mastery of death (Rom. 6:9). Based on our being "raised up with Christ" (Eph. 2:6; Col. 2:12; 3:1), Paul was desirous that Christians know "the surpassing greatness of the power" (Eph. 1:19) that is functioning with us as Christians, the very "working of the strength of His might which He brought about in Christ when He raised Him from the dead" (Eph. 1:20). This is the "power of His resurrection" (Phil. 3:10) that Paul continually longed to know and experience in a deeper way.

The writer of the epistle to the Hebrews refers to "the better resurrection" (Heb. 11:35) that is in Christ alone, whereby "the God of peace who raised up...Jesus our Lord, equips us in every good thing to do His will, working in us that which is pleasing in His sight, through Jesus Christ" (Heb. 13:20,21).

Consistent with the other New Testament writers, Peter posits the resurrection as the prerequisite and personal reality of Christ's life received in spiritual regeneration, when we are "born again to a living hope through the resurrection of Jesus Christ from the dead" (I Peter 1:3). This is the basis on which we are "saved...through the resurrection of Jesus Christ" (I Peter 3:21).

When the Apostle John refers to "passing out of death into life" (John 5:24; I John 3:14), it is the resurrection reality that is foundational to his thought, implemented "because He has given us of His Spirit" (I John 4:13).

Everything in the New Testament, the entirety of Christian preaching and theology, is predicated on the Resurrection of Jesus and the continuing dynamic of His life in those who receive Him by faith. The great Scottish preacher, James S. Stewart, expressed it so eloquently when he wrote,

> "The resurrection was indeed the very core of the apostolic *kerygma*. ...It was the theme of every Christian sermon; it was the master-motive of every act of Christian evangelism; and not one line of the New Testament was written – not one sentence, whether of Gospels, Epistles, Acts or Apocalypse, was penned apart from the conviction that He of whom these things were being written had conquered death and was alive for ever.
>
> "Never did the apostles make the mistake, all too common today, of regarding the Resurrection as a mere epilogue to the Gospel, an addendum to the scheme of salvation, a providential afterthought of God, a codicil to the divine last will and testament. This is to falsify disastrously the whole emphasis of the Bible. Not as an appendix to the faith was the Resurrection ever preached in the apostolic Church. The one and only God the apostles worshipped was the God of the Resurrection. The one and only Gospel they were commissioned to preach was the overpowering, magnificent good news of the Resurrection." [11]

Can the emphasis be made any more evident than it is made throughout the New Testament that the Resurrection of Jesus is not just an historical event of yesteryear or just an anticipation of embodiment in the future, but is the essence of the vital restoration of humanity in the present? The misemphases in modern Christian religion necessitate a call for Resurrection Theology that returns to the Biblical emphasis.

We cannot do better than to allow the Scottish preacher to continue to drive home his point:

"It is immensely significant that those first Christians never preached the resurrection simply as Jesus' escape from the grave, the reanimation of One who had died, the return of the Master to His friends. The always proclaimed it as the living God in omnipotent action. [12]

"This is the conviction that makes the New Testament...the most exciting and the most relevant book in the world. The power that was strong enough to get Jesus out of the grave, and thus to set going the whole Christian movement across the centuries, mighty enough to shatter and confound the hideous demonic alliance of evil, creative enough to smite death with resurrection – this power is in action still. [13]

"...preaching the Resurrection means telling men that the identical divine energy which at the first took Christ out of the grave is available still – available not only at journey's end to save them in the hour of death, but available here and now to cause them to live.

It is an awful catastrophe for the Church when the proclamation of such a Gospel grows – pity us – dull and listless and mechanical. ...the same power which on that day shattered death is now given us for life – to vitalize the most depressed and disillusioned and defeated son of man into a resurrected personality and a conquering soul." [14]

"How was it that a little group of men in an upper room – ordinary, fallible, blundering men – became the nucleus of a movement that was to turn the world upside down? This was the Church's hidden secret. It was not that they were commanding personalities; most of them were not. It was not that they had official backing, impressive credentials, or illustrious patronage: of all that they had less than nothing. It was this – that the unearthly power which at the first had brought creation into being, which now at the last had inaugurated a new creation in the Resurrection of Christ, had laid hold upon them and refashioned their lives as with a second birth." [15]

"it is no mere interest in immortality which explains the apostolic concentration on the Resurrection. It was not as a dramatic verification of personal survival that they preached Christ risen from the dead. They were not really concerned with proofs and theories of survival as such.

> "It was the shattering of history by a creative act of God Almighty. God was doing something comparable only with what He had done at the first creation. This was the beginning of a new era for the universe, the decisive turning-point for the human race. ...In the resurrection the new age had arrived, and this stupendous miracle signified the storming of history and the transforming of the world."[16]

> "The Resurrection was evidence that there had now appeared, in the midst of time, life of a new dimension and the baptism of eternity. The heralds of the Resurrection were not merely preaching it as a fact: they were living in it as in a new country. They had received a Kingdom which could not be shaken."[17]

Preach on Dr. Stewart! The impact of the resurrection cannot be overstated or overrated. The Resurrection of Jesus Christ is THE most stupendous act of God's grace. It is the focal point of all human history. It is the transforming reality in light of which everything else must be interpreted. All meaningful human existence must be interpreted by the earth-shattering, death-defeating, history-defining reality of Jesus' Resurrection.

Christianity is not a message of merely what "has been" (past) and "will be" (future); it is the message of what "is", the vital dynamic of the resurrected "I AM" of God who restores the whole of creation. The Resurrection facilitates and is the personal dynamic of the restoration of humanity whereby God functions once again in man by the presence of His own divine life in the Christian.

Christian theology is not simply an ideological and epistemological construct concerning events and doctrines. The personal resurrection-presence of the living Lord Jesus is intrinsic to His teaching. They cannot be detached. Apart from His resurrection there is no validity to His teaching. This is why Thomas F. Torrance writes, "What Jesus Christ is in His resurrection, He is in Himself. The very life of Jesus is the content of the resurrection." [18]

Conclusion

Resurrection theology is necessarily Resurrection-living, the living manifestation of the life and character of the risen Lord Jesus in Christian behavior. As such, this is also a call for Resurrection-community, whereby the church functions as the Body of Christ by the interpersonal interaction of people living by the Resurrection-life of Jesus, loving one another and seeking the other's highest good.

The Resurrection is the basis of everything that can legitimately be called "Christian." It is only by the indwelling activity of the risen Lord Jesus that the dynamic life of Christ continues to effect Christianity.

Apart from the Resurrection there is no Christianity. Apart from the Resurrection there is no gospel. Apart from the Resurrection there is no spiritual life. Apart from the Resurrection there is no salvation. Apart from the Resurrection there is no righteousness, holiness or godliness. Apart from the Resurrection there is no Christian living. Apart from the Resurrection there is no hope. It is imperative that we articulate and proclaim Resurrection Theology.

ENDNOTES

1 Geffré, Claude, *A New Age in Theology*. New York: Paulist Press. 1974. pg. 1.

2 Brinsmead, Robert D., Verdict Essay 1E, "The Resurrection", April, 1999. pg. 20.

3 Stewart, James S., *A Man in Christ: The Vital Elements of St. Paul's Religion.* Grand Rapids: Baker Book House. pg. 135.

4 *Ibid.,* pg. 136.

5 Kunneth, Walter, *The Theology of the Resurrection*. St. Louis: Concordia Publishing House. 1965. pg. 294.

6 Morison, Frank, *Who Moved the Stone?* London: Faber and Faber Limited. 1930.

7 McDowell, Josh, *The Resurrection Factor.* San Bernardino: Here's Life Publishers. 1981.

8 Brinsmead, Robert D., *op. cit.*, pg. 2.

9 Geffré, Claude, *op. cit.*, pg. 1

10 Williams, H. A., *True Resurrection.* New York: Holt, Rinehart and Winston. 1972. pgs 4,5.

11 Stewart, James S., *A Faith to Proclaim.* New York: Charles Scribner's Sons. 1953. pgs. 104,105.

12 Stewart, James S., *King For Ever.* London: Hodder and Stoughton. pg. 142.

13 *Ibid.,* pg. 143.

14 Stewart, James S., *A Faith to Proclaim.* pg. 126.

15 *Ibid.,* pg. 127.

16 *Ibid.,* pg. 106,107

17 *Ibid.,* pg. 109.

18 Torrance, Thomas F., *Space, Time and Resurrection.* Grand Rapids: William B. Eerdmans Publishing Co. 1976.

CHRISTIANITY *IS* RESURRECTION

The gospel is the message of the resurrection. The Gospel IS resurrection. Christianity is the expression of the resurrection. Christianity *IS* resurrection. Someone might say: "But Christianity is Christ!" That is true, but Jesus Christ said, "I AM the Resurrection and the life" (John 11:25). Jesus Christ is the content, the essence of resurrection-life. Jesus never said, "I AM the Cross", but He did say, "I AM the resurrection". The resurrection is the expression of the dynamic of all that Jesus IS. In fact, the resurrection is the reality of all that Christianity IS. The vital understanding of everything that is Christian is in the resurrection. Resurrection-life is the focal point of all Christian teaching – the starting point from which everything must be appraised, evaluated and interpreted – EVERYTHING! Everything prior in time, time itself, and everything that follows chronologically, logically and theologically can only correctly be understood in light of the resurrection; all human history, all human thought.

Many have expressed this centrality of Christian teaching in the resurrection:

> "One's whole theology is determined by one's view of the resurrection."[1]
>
> "All Christian doctrines do nothing more or less than manifest some facet of the basic affirmation of the resurrection.[2]
>
> "Justification, adoption, sanctification and glorification, as applied to believers, are derived from the significance of the resurrection.[3]

> "The resurrection is the first and last and dominating element in the Christian consciousness of the New Testament."[4]
>
> "All New Testament facts have to be broached from the key position of the resurrection. Paul's thinking in all his utterances rotates around one unifying centre, and that centre is the raising of Christ from the dead."[5]
>
> "The raising of Christ is THE act of God, whose significance is not to be compared with any event before or after. It is the primal datum of theology, from which there can be no abstracting, and the normative presupposition for every valid dogmatic judgment and for the meaningful construction of a Christian theology. Thus, the resurrection of Jesus becomes the Archimedean point for theology. All theological statements are oriented in one way or another toward this focal point. There is no Christian knowledge of God which does not acquire its ultimate fullness and depth from a revelation of God in the Risen One."[6]

All of history, and especially Biblical history, must be interpreted by the resurrection. Those who preceded the resurrection were who they were, and did what they did, because of what was, Who was, to happen in the resurrection.

But the resurrection is so totally different from any other historical fact, that it cannot be considered by the same guidelines or criteria of circumstantial evidence. It is beyond historical categories. All else must be considered in the light of, in the context of, the resurrection. If the resurrection of Jesus were just another historical miracle, then Christianity is but a dead religion! In the resurrection God breaks into history; eternity breaks into time; God re-creates humanity; God establishes the social order He intended.

Christianity IS resurrection. At Easter time, we do not just celebrate another event in history – even if it be regarded as the greatest event in history. Resurrection is not just an historical event; it is an on-going dynamic of the life of God in Jesus Christ. We do not just assent to the historicity or theological accuracy of the resurrection of Jesus Christ; we encounter resurrection. We encounter and have personal relationship with the One who is "the resurrection and the life." (John 11:25). One cannot count themselves a "Christian" unless they have encountered, received, and are participating in the resurrection life of Jesus Christ.

In order to demonstrate that resurrection is that which constitutes all of that which is called "Christian", I want to consider several categories, both chronological and theological, that can only be properly understood by the reality of the resurrection:

Chronological Categories

(1) CREATION. To attempt to understand creation – God's bringing into being of the world – apart from the resurrection of Jesus Christ, may cause one to arrive at Shakespeare's conclusion: "All the world's a stage, and all the men and women merely players...; "Life's but a walking shadow, a poor player that struts and frets his hour upon the stage, and then is heard no more; It is a tale told by an idiot, full of sound and fury, signifying nothing." Creation has no direction apart from the resurrection. To view creation apart from resurrection is to arrive at either evolutionary hodge-podge or at the rigid formulas of "creationism," and both are just as meaningless. Man as mere potentiality is not an exalted view of his createdness.

Creation is invested with meaning only when we look back at it from the perspective of resurrection. Jesus Christ was active in creation as Creator (John 1:3: Col. 1:16); as the indwelling presence of the Divine character that was to be visibly expressed, i.e. imaged, in man (Gen. 1:26,27). The initial Genesis creation "set the stage" for the "new creation" brought into being in Jesus Christ (Gal. 6:16). By the resurrection of Jesus Christ, we have the fulfilment of creation, the re-creation of a new functional humanity (Eph. 2:15), wherein the "image" is restored so that the Divine character might be expressed in righteousness and holiness (Eph. 4:24).

A Christian understanding of creation must take into account the resurrection.

(2) FALL OF MAN. If the Fall of man is taken as the starting point of one's theological understanding, then righting the wrong of sin becomes the end-objective. If our theology begins in Genesis chapter 3, then it will conclude at the cross, and be nothing more than a "Mr. Fix-It Theology."

Only when we consider the Fall of man from the perspective of the resurrection, do we understand the active energizing of death by the devil (Heb. 2:14), the extent to which the unregenerate are "slaves of sin" (John 8:34), and the radical spiritual exchange of conversion when men turn from the dominion of Satan to God (Acts 26:18).

The Fall of man can only be understood from a Christian point of view by looking backwards from the resurrection and the restoration of life therein.

(3) ISRAEL. Apart from the resurrection we might conclude with Norman Ewer, "How odd of God, to choose the Jews." The Jewish people, the nation of Israel; they were not faithful and obedient. They were selfish, idolatrous, nationalistic and racist. If they are to be regarded, unconditionally, as "God's chosen people", then God might well be represented as a racist God, a God who is a "respecter of persons" (Acts 10:34).

Looking back at Israel in the Old Testament from a resurrection perspective, we understand that they were a "picture-people" intended to illustrate what God was to do in the resurrection in raising up a people for His own possession, a chosen race, a royal priesthood, a holy nation (I Peter 2:9). The physical Israel of the Old Testament represented a people "set apart" to function as intended, but they failed to thus function because of unbelief and disobedience (Heb. 3:16-4:6). By the resurrection of Jesus all Christians become the "Israel of God" (Gal. 6:16; Rom. 9:6); people "set apart" to function as intended; people who can collectively be called "Israel" because we have fought with God, surrendered to God and been conquered by God, spiritually.

The resurrection gives us an eternal perspective of who the people of Israel really are.

(4) PROPHETS. If the prophets of the Old Testament are considered apart from the resurrection of Jesus, they might indeed appear to be "blowing in the wind," as Bob Dylan sang. Apart from the spiritual implications of the resurrection they would be rambling rabble-rousers, mere doomsday sayers; and much of what they said would not have come true – they would be false-prophets!

Much of what the prophets said requires the resurrection to make any sense. The prophets of the Old Testament saw glimpses, both of the resurrection itself (Acts 2:31) and the many implications thereof: that He would be king on the throne of David (Ezekiel 37:24,25; Luke 1:32,33), that He would be a light to the Gentiles (Acts 13:47,48), etc.

The prophets of the Old Testament cannot be properly understood except from a resurrection perspective.

(5) INCARNATION. To attempt to contemplate the incarnation of Jesus Christ apart from the resurrection will simply boggle the human mind. Discussion of hypostatic union and kenotic theories are but "dead ends" if the incarnation does not lead to something more than an unexplainable historical phenomena of One who is inexplicably both God and man in one person. The apologist's alternatives of regarding the historical Jesus as either a "liar" or a "lunatic" would be the only logical choices.

The resurrection invests the incarnation with a fullness of meaning that points to the incarnation of God in all mankind. "God was in Christ" (II Cor. 5:19), and by the resurrected-life of Jesus can dwell in every man. "The Word became flesh" (John 1:14) in Jesus, and God wants to be manifested in the flesh of all Christians (II Cor. 4:11). Jesus was "Emmanuel" (Matt. 1:23), and God intended to be with and in everyone who would receive the resurrection dynamic of Christ by faith.

The incarnation becomes a prototype of deity functioning within humanity when viewed through its universal fulfilment in the resurrection.

(6) LIFE OF JESUS. From an historical perspective that fails to account for the resurrection, the life of Jesus here on earth was but an incomparable ideal and an impossible example. If Jesus lived the life that He lived simply because He was God, deity, something that no mortal man can be, then His matchless moral example simply condemns us all the more.

By the resurrection we come to appreciate the dynamic that made the life of Jesus what it was. He lived by the Life of Another - He let God be God in Him for every moment in time for thirty-three years. "I do nothing of My own initiative," He said, "The Father abiding in Me does His works" (John 14:10). Even His miracles were but what God did through Him (Acts 2:22). Thus, He modelled the life of a man, normal humanity, a man who let God be God in a man, man as God intended. By resurrection He makes that same dynamic of life available to Christians.

The behavioral expression of the life of Jesus here on earth is only encouraging to us today because of the resurrection. The life lived once in Christ can be lived in us.

(7) CRUCIFIXION. The emphasis on the Cross has often been allowed to usurp the centrality of the resurrection in Christian teaching. To divorce the cross from the resurrection is to develop a "gospel of gore", a bloody religion that is ghastly and grotesque. The death emphasis of the cross leads to masochistic forms of flagellation, be they physical or psychological ("death to self"). To consider the Cross apart from the resurrection is the springboard for innumerable theories of the atonement, but it creates a most negative and sin-conscious religion. In fact the detachment of the crucifixion from the resurrection diminishes the vicarious and sacrificial elements of the Lamb slain for the sins of the world.

The crucifixion of Christ on the cross of Calvary is not an end in itself. It was but a remedial action, to remedy the problem of the death consequences of man's sin. The problems of sin and death and Satan's dominion were remedied at the cross. God then made His Life available to mankind by the resurrection. On the cross, Jesus exclaimed, "It is Finished!" (John 19:30); He saw ahead to the completed work of God in the resurrection. Whenever Paul refers to "the word of the cross" (I Cor. 1:18; Gal. 6:14), and preaching "Christ crucified" (I Cor. 2:2), He always does so from the perspective of the "finished work" of the resurrection.

The crucifixion postulates but a popular martyr-hero unless it is invested with meaning by the resurrection, wherein the crucifixion becomes God's "No" to death and sin, and the resurrection becomes God's "Yes" to Life for all mankind.

(8) PENTECOST. Apart from the full import of the resurrection, the Pentecost experience recorded in Acts chapter two becomes but an initiation demonstration at the commencement of the church. Many mistakenly look back to Pentecost as the necessary expression of ecstatic utterances and *glossalalia* that is to be indicative of all genuine Christian experience. Pentecost becomes the event when God distributed His gifts, trophies and "power-toys."

Only by an understanding of the resurrection can Pentecost be properly understood as the out-pouring of the Spirit of the resurrected Jesus. The Spirit of Christ (Rom. 8:9) was made available to indwell all mankind who would receive Him by faith. The risen Lord Jesus in spiritual form came to empower Christian people (Rom. 1:4; Eph. 1:19,20) at Pentecost. This is what accounts for the impact of the early church on the world around it: they lived like they did, and did what they did, by the resurrection-power of the Spirit of Christ within them.

Pentecost must be viewed as a demonstration of the availability of resurrection.

(9) SECOND COMING. The Second Coming of Jesus to earth is so often interpreted apart from the resurrection implications. By the resurrection, Jesus was raised to reign on the spiritual throne of David over the spiritual kingdom of God. Many deny these resurrection realities and believe that Jesus will come again to establish a physical kingdom, having failed to become a priest-king the first time He came. They have sacrificed the resurrection to crass materialistic, nationalistic and racial expectations.

When viewed in the light of the resurrection, the second coming of Jesus becomes the glorious consummation of God's spiritual kingdom. Maranatha! Come Lord Jesus.

(10) END OF TIME. The end of time when considered apart from the resurrection, will indeed be meaningless and purposeless. That is why "nihilism" has become such a prominent idea -- the philosophy of "nothingness" -- that nothing makes sense, it all amounts to nothing. Others look to the end of time as but the opportunity to break the cycle of meaningless life, to get "off the wheel" and to be obliterated into the nothingness of Nirvana. Such viewpoints are devoid of the hope that is in the resurrection alone.

From the perspective of Christ's resurrection, the end of time is the consummation of time when Christians glory in the eternality of the new heaven and the new earth, and the unhindered enjoyment of the eternal life that is ours already in the resurrection of Jesus Christ.

Theological Categories

Now let us consider the resurrection implications in various theological categories:

(1) REDEMPTION. To consider the redemption of God in Jesus Christ apart from the resurrection is to sell it short of the price paid. Redemption means to "buy back" with the payment of a price. It was the terminology of the slave market in Biblical times. But to be bought out of slavery with a ransom payment, is not enough if we are not emancipated, set free, liberated. Redemption without resurrection is to be "bought with a price" (I Cor. 6:20) -- the ransom price of Christ's death on the cross -- but to disregard the emancipation.

It is by the resurrection that we are "set free, so as not to be subject again to a yoke of slavery" (Gal. 5:1). The resurrection establishes the glorious objective of redemption. We are bought with a price in order to be all that God intended man to be; redeemed for God's use and expression of His glorious character in functional humanity.

The resurrection invests redemption with the full content of its purchase price.

(2) REGENERATION. There is so much talk about being "born again" in religious circles today, but much of it is bankrupt because it does not incorporate the resurrection. For some, being "born again" is a renaissance of one's thinking, a re-orientation of one's life, or a subjective experience of heart-felt rejuvenation. Apart from the resurrection, regeneration is as absurd a concept as it was to Nicodemus in John chapter three, where Jesus' mention of "born again" conjured up mental images of an obstetric return to the womb of his mother.

The resurrection is the reality that invests regeneration with meaning. Jesus was raised from the dead, life out of death, in order that we might be "raised to newness of life" (Rom. 6:4) in Christ Jesus. Jesus IS the resurrection and the life (John 11:25) with which (Whom) we are re-lifed spiritually in regeneration. (John 14:6; Col. 3:4). Regeneration is not facilitated by the cross, but rather by the resurrection. I Peter 1:3 - "Blessed be the God and Father of our Lord Jesus Christ, who according to His great mercy has caused us to be born again to a living hope through the resurrection of Jesus Christ from the dead."

Regeneration is a re-genesis, bringing man into being again spiritually, rebreathing into man the "breath of life" (Genesis 2:7). Thus, we become a new creature in Christ (II Cor. 5:17), a "new man" (Eph. 4:24; Col. 3:10) with the image of God restored in man. Regeneration is the resurrection-life of Jesus brought into being in the Christian.

(3) JUSTIFICATION. "Justification" is a Biblical word that has been much confused and misunderstood by Christians because it has been defined apart from the resurrection. The popular explanation is that God, the heavenly Judge sits in His heavenly courtroom, and when a person believes in His Son, Jesus Christ, the Judge bangs down His gavel, saying, "Declared righteous!" Thus, justification becomes a legal acquittal, a word of pardon, the non-imputation of sin, "just-as-if-I'd" never sinned. But the declaration is regarded as a legal fiction which is on the heavenly accounting books, having no practical effect in terms of behavioral righteousness in one's life today.

The resurrection invests justification with practical implications for Christian behavior today. The Risen One is the Righteous One - Jesus Christ. Paul indicates in Romans 4:25 that Jesus "was raised for our justification." The resurrection-life of Jesus that comes to dwell in us when the Spirit of Christ is in our spirit (Rom. 8:16), is righteous-life. We are "made righteous" (Rom. 5:19); we become the "righteousness of God in Christ" (II Cor 5:21); Christ Jesus becomes to us righteousness (I Cor. 1:30). The righteous character of the Righteous God is actualized in us by the resurrection-life of Jesus.

Justification requires the living content of resurrection in order to be properly understood.

(4) SALVATION. Salvation has been trivialized by its separation from the resurrection in contemporary evangelical theology. Salvation separated from the resurrection is conceived of as but a rescue from the results of sin or a "fire insurance policy" from the effects of hell. Likewise, salvation apart from the resurrection dynamic is regarded as but a commodity of "eternal life" which one can "possess" by reason of one's attestation of the historicity and doctrine of Jesus Christ; a spiritual benefit dispensed by a benefactor. Salvation apart from resurrection is merely preventative or beneficient.

Only when salvation is understood in the on-going continuity of the resurrection-life of Jesus Christ, only then does salvation remain connected with the work of the eternal Savior. Salvation does "make safe" from the dysfunctional humanity enslaved to sin, but Christians are saved unto the functional humanity of the Savior and Lord, Jesus Christ living through us. We are "saved by His life" (Rom. 5:10), as the resurrection-life of Jesus, the "saving life of Christ" is operative in our behavior.

The resurrection gives salvation a positive vitality, which is far more than escapism.

(5) GRACE. Because resurrection has been absent from evangelical conceptions of grace, the grace of God has been relegated to merely "redemptive grace" (God's Redemption At Christ's Expense) or the threshold factor of "saving grace." When grace is thus interpreted as static event or experience, it is then dispensed with for any practical purpose, and gives way to law, legalism and the performance of self-effort. The Christian life is regarded by many Christians as a life of performance, commitment and involvement.

The Grace-life of Christianity can only be understood in the context of the resurrection. The free-flow of God's activity is made operative in Christian lives by the resurrection of Jesus Christ. The Christian life is the resurrection-grace-life. Paul says, "I am who I am by the grace of God" (I Cor. 15:10). The Christian life is all of grace or it is not Christian life.

(6) FAITH. Faith, apart from resurrection becomes but mental assent to a belief system, or dogmatic assertions of the veracity of propositional truth from the Book. Worse yet, faith may be regarded as superstitious expectations which are no more than "faith in faith."

Biblical faith can only be understood and exercised in the context of resurrection-grace. Faith is the response of reliance on the resurrection dynamic of God in Christ. Faith is our receptivity to His resurrection activity.

(7) SANCTIFICATION. Sanctification, apart from resurrection, will inevitably be conceived in terms of externals. It may be the externals of attire and possessions, avoiding what appears "worldly" and utilizing the out-dated that appears more "spiritual." Sanctification is sometimes regarded as the impossible ideal of a perfect life to be lived by imitating the life of Jesus Christ. Sanctification is most often conceived of as behavior governed by morality and ethics, the codification of behavior into rules and regulations, techniques and formulas, how-tos; the legalistic conformity to which is regarded as holiness.

Sanctification can only be understood and experienced by the resurrection-life of Jesus. It is the process of allowing the holy character of God to be lived out in our behavior as the Risen Lord Jesus lives out His life through us. It is the "life of Jesus manifested in our mortal bodies" (II Cor. 4:10). Sanctification is resurrection-living!

(8) HOLY SPIRIT. Considerations of the Holy Spirit apart from the resurrection either "box" Him into a theological box as "the third person of the Godhead," or set Him up as a spiritual "stimulant", a power-force, that is available as a super-spiritual experience, subsequent to receiving Jesus Christ in regeneration.

The Holy Spirit cannot be properly understood in the life of the Christian apart from the resurrection. The Holy Spirit is the Spirit of Christ, the Spirit of the Risen Lord Jesus. Paul writes in II Cor. 3:17, "Now the Lord is the Spirit; and where the Spirit of the Lord is, there is liberty." The Holy Spirit is present in the spirit of every genuine Christian (Rom. 8:16), to express the resurrection-life of Jesus Christ in character and activity.

(9) CHURCH. Apart from the resurrection-dynamic of Jesus Christ, the Church becomes a mere historical or theological society for further discussion of the same. Sometimes it becomes a fellowship of like-minded believers, gathering for subjective "worship" experiences. When the church becomes a social organization or religious institution it binds people up in the absolutism, authoritarianism and activism of religion.

Only on the basis of the resurrection does the Church become the collective Body of the life of the Risen Lord Jesus. The church is intended to be the collective expression and interactions of those "called-out" to function in resurrection-life; Jesus Christ living in resurrection community, the inaugurated kingdom of God, the fulfilment of the Israel of God (Gal. 6:16; Rom. 9:6).

(10) ESCHATOLOGY. When the resurrection-dynamic of Jesus Christ is misunderstood, then the consideration of "last things" often degenerates into mere speculative "futurism," with their voluminous linear time-lines and charts. On the other hand, it may become a campaign of social reform to create a "new world order."

When Christians understand the resurrection, then the consideration of "last things", i.e. eschatology, is not "utopianism." By the resurrection of Jesus Christ, God has established the "last things", the "last days". Jesus Christ is the "first and the last", the "alpha and the omega", the Creator and the End. All that God has designed for man is inaugurated and realized in Jesus Christ, and that by the resurrection.

Christianity IS resurrection, the resurrection dynamic and Life of Jesus Christ operative in everything. The resurrection is not just an historical or theological fact to be believed; He is a living Person to be received by faith, moment by moment in every situation of our existence. Jesus said, "I AM the Resurrection and the Life" (John 11:25), and the implications of that are beyond the abilities of human contemplation.

Christianity IS Resurrection, because Jesus IS Resurrection and Life. Oh, that those who call themselves "Christians" today might understand what it meant for Jesus to be raised from the dead on that first Easter morning. It was Eternity intersecting into time with "eternal life." It was God re-creating humanity and society. It was God interpreting all of history. It was God in Christ bringing Life to a world dead in sin.

Christianity IS Resurrection. Have you received resurrection? Are you enjoying resurrection?

ENDNOTES

1 Runia, Klaas, *Christianity Today,* March 17, 1967., article entitled "The Third Day He Rose Again."
2 Chirico, P. F.,
3 Gaffin, Richard P., *Resurrection and Redemption*.
4 Denney, James,
5 Kunneth, Walter, *The Theology of the Resurrection*.
6 Torrance, T.F., *Space, Time and Resurrection.* pg, 74.

"It is the Resurrection that is being by-passed"

It has been many years since I first read a statement in Thomas F. Torrance's book, *Space, Time and Resurrection* – a statement that has reverberated and resonated in my mind ever since that first reading. In the context of writing about "the Resurrection and Justification", Torrance asserts,

> "When, therefore, the Protestant doctrine of justification is formulated only in terms of forensic imputation of righteousness or the non-imputation of sins in such a way as to avoid saying that to justify is to make righteous, *it is the resurrection that is being bypassed.*" (page 63) (italics added)

The last phrase of that sentence kept ringing in my mind: "*it is the resurrection that is being bypassed.*"

After much pondering of that phrase, I have determined to elaborate and amplify the implications of that statement beyond just the context of justification to which Torrance referred.

Since the resurrection of Jesus Christ is the keystone that gives living dynamic to everything Christian, it is impossible to be exhaustive in noting everything that by-passes resurrection life. Every aberration, every divergent emphasis of Christianity will necessarily fail to take into account Jesus as "the resurrection and the life" (John 11:25). So, all we can do is to begin to note how the resurrection is by-passed, and allow this to become an ever-expanding list.

It is the resurrection that is being by-passed when the incarnation of Jesus is celebrated only as a "birthday party for Jesus," and Christians are battling for the right to construct nativity scenes in public places, rather than seeing, in the light of the resurrection, that the living Lord Jesus is to be incarnated, i.e. enfleshed in us, as His life and character manifested in our mortal bodies (II Cor. 4:10,11).

It is the resurrection that is being by-passed when humanistic anthropological concepts are allowed to creep into Christian thinking in varying forms of "evangelical humanism" that accept the self-potentiality of man to self-generate his own character, rather than recognizing that Christian character is derived only from the Risen Christ, and that "apart from Him, we can do nothing" (John 15:5).

It is the resurrection that is being by-passed when the Christian gospel is conceptualized as an ideological and epistemological belief-system of historical and theological data whereby the fundamental facts are properly, logical and authoritatively interpreted, rather than receiving the "good news" as the ontological Being of the risen life of Jesus, the Personified Truth (John 14:6).

It is the resurrection that is being by-passed when Christianity is viewed as a Book-religion that determines all matters by the authority of the Bible as the Word of God and elevates the Scriptures as the sole agency of the Spirit, rather than accepting the Resurrected Lord as having "all authority in heaven and earth" (Matt. 28:18), and the One in whom life is found (John 5:39,40).

It is the resurrection that is being by-passed when God's Law is perceived as eternally viable rules and regulations, precepts and principles to regulate human behavior and reconstruct national society, rather than the living dynamic of the Risen Christ written in our hearts (Heb. 8:10; 10:16) to express divine character through our behavior by the "law of Christ" (I Cor. 9:21; Gal. 6:2).

It is the resurrection that is being by-passed when the redemptive efficacy of the cross becomes the focal point of Christian teaching, emphasizing death instead of life, even personifying the "cross" and the "blood" as having continued redemptive or sanctifying efficacy, rather than proclaiming the "finished work" (John 19:30) of Jesus Christ, whereby we have been "crucified with Christ" (Rom. 6:6; Gal. 2:20).

It is the resurrection that is being by-passed when sin, guilt, and the "lusts of the flesh" occupy one's thinking and teaching in an emphasis on sin-consciousness and confessionalism, rather than praising God for the resurrection-victory that is ours in Christ Jesus (I Cor. 15;57), and relying on the Risen One who has set us free from the law of sin and death (Rom. 8:2).

It is the resurrection that is being by-passed when salvation is portrayed as a fire-insurance policy, or as a conversion commodity dispensed by a separated Savior culminating in a false assurance of "once saved, always saved," rather than our being "saved by the life" (Rom. 5:10) of the Risen Lord allowing us to be "made safe" to function as God intended by the resurrection-life of Jesus Christ.

It is the resurrection that is being by-passed when justification (as Torrance noted) is cast only as a legal and forensic declaration of right-ness with God in the heavenly courtroom, based on the imputed benefits of

Christ's action, rather than the righteousness for which Christ was raised (Rom. 4:25) in order that Christians might be "made righteous" (Rom. 5:19; I Cor. 1:30; II Cor. 5:21) by His indwelling presence and living expression of the "fruit of righteousness" (Eph. 5:9; Phil. 1:11).

It is the resurrection that is being by-passed when reconciliation with God is objectified as but a bringing together of alienated parties so that they can coexist in conciliation, rather than a relational reconciliation wherein the "I AM" of the resurrected Jesus (John 11:25) enters into spiritual union with the Christian (I Cor. 6:17), and reconciles all things to Himself (Col. 1:20).

It is the resurrection that is being by-passed when regeneration is understood only as an initial experience of conversion-birthing in order to renew one's attempts to please God, rather than the resurrection objective (I Peter 1:3) whereby we pass from death to life (John 5:24; I John 3:14) and are raised to newness of life (Rom. 6:4,5) in Christ (Eph. 2:6; Col. 2:12; 3:1).

It is the resurrection that is being by-passed when faith is identified only as mental assent to an historical Jesus, or correct belief in factual data that is Scripturally accurate, rather than the receptivity of Christ's resurrection-activity whereby we walk (Col. 2:6) and conduct our lives deriving from His life, allowing for the out-working of His life (James 2:19,26).

It is the resurrection that is being by-passed when God's grace is explained merely as the "undeserved favor" of God that initiated the incarnation and crucifixion of Jesus, or as the "threshold factor" of the Christian life, rather than the divine dynamic of God's activity by the Risen Son in Christians, being "the grace in which we stand" (Rom. 5:2)

It is the resurrection that is being by-passed when Christian living is encouraged via legalistic actions of performance and "works", as moralistic virtues, or as the imitation of Jesus' example, rather than Jesus Christ, the Risen One, living out His life in the Christian (II Cor. 13:5; Gal. 2:20; Col. 1:27).

It is the resurrection that is being by-passed when sanctification and holiness are alleged to be facilitated by separation from designated sinful activities, or by a subsequent "second blessing" of God's grace, rather than the resurrected Christ functioning as the Spirit of holiness (Rom. 1:4) and manifesting the holy character of God in Christian behavior that we might share His holiness (Heb. 12:10).

It is the resurrection that is being by-passed when the Lordship of Christ is depicted as a secondary and subsequent commitment to discipleship, an optional submission of the Christian, rather than the right of the Risen Lord in the believer to function as the Lord that He is (Acts 2:36) by the Spirit (II Cor. 3:17) in authoritative control of our lives.

It is the resurrection that is being by-passed when the Holy Spirit is emphasized as the power-source of supernatural manifestations detached from the living Christ, rather than as the Spirit of Christ (Romans 8:9), the life-giving Spirit (I Cor. 15:45) of the Risen Lord who is the Spirit (II Cor. 3:16,17) and gives us His life by His own indwelling person (Rom. 8:11).

It is the resurrection that is being by-passed when the Kingdom of God, kingdom of heaven, or kingdom of Christ is regarded only, or primarily, as a future realm that is the object of Christian hope, rather than the resurrection-reign of the risen Lord Jesus within us (Luke 17:21) into which all Christians have been transferred (Col. 1:13) and now participate in by the Holy Spirit (Rom. 14:17) while still expecting the continuum of that kingdom in the future.

It is the resurrection that is being by-passed when the Church of Jesus Christ is viewed as an organizational institution to be run like a business with the latest marketing techniques, and its success evaluated by the statistical analysis of the numerical "bottom-line," rather than the resurrection-community comprised of all believers in whom the Risen One lives, functioning as a living organism, the Body of Christ (Col. 1:18,24), ministering to one another in love (Rom. 5:5).

It is the resurrection that is being by-passed when ecclesiastical purity is evaluated by doctrinal and behavioral correctness leading to denominationalism, sectarianism, and separation from those with differing opinions or behavioral liberties, rather than the purity of the character of the Risen Lord expressed in Christian behavior, whereby we recognize our oneness in Christ (John 17:21), the unity of the Spirit in the bond of peace (Eph. 4:3-6).

It is the resurrection that is being by-passed when eschatology (last things) is regarded as the future fulfillment of God's yet-unfulfilled promises, rather than the living dynamic of the "Last Adam" (I Cor. 15:45) in the "last days" (Acts 2:17; Heb. 1:2) wherein the resurrection-life of Jesus fulfills all God's promises (II Cor. 1:20).

It is the resurrection that is being by-passed when millennial expectations desire to see Jesus return for a physical and earthly reign of 1000 years worshiping in a rebuilt temple in Jerusalem, rather than recognizing the completion and fullness of Christ's work whereby He reigns as the Risen Lord in His people today.

It is the resurrection that is being by-passed when heaven is conceived as a place out there, a perfect utopia reserved for the future where Christians will collect their deserved rewards, rather than the presence of a perfect

God who has blessed us with every spiritual blessing in heavenly places (Eph. 1:3) that we might participate in the "kingdom of heaven" (Matt. 4:17 by the indwelling of the Perfect Risen Jesus Christ.

It is the resurrection that is being by-passed whenever we fail to recognize the full import of how God has restored humanity by the raising of His Son, Jesus Christ, whereby His "finished work" continues to bring to pass all that God intends to accomplish by His grace.

Other Books by Jim Fowler

Man As God Intended: A Study in Theological Anthropology. This book, the first that Jim wrote, lays the foundation for the remainder of his writing and teaching. The themes of theological anthropology, derivative humanity, and Christocentric theology are introduced in this book. Though filled with theological content, it is written in an easy-to-understand manner that will not intimidate the reader. If you haven't read Jim's writings before, this is a good place to start.

Christ at Work in You: The Continuing Function of the Risen Lord Jesus. This volume is a good sequel to *Man as God Intended*, for it transitions from the theological groundwork of the indwelling Lord Jesus to the practical outworking of Christ's life in our daily lives. Jim considers the inevitable behavioral conflict of the Spirit and the flesh (cf. Gal. 5:16-18), explaining that the "flesh" pertains to the residual selfish and sinful patterns that remain in the soul of a Christian.

Spirit-union Allows for Soul-rest. Beginning with the recognition of the Christian's spirit-union with the livng Lord Jesus (cf. I Cor. 6:17), this volume explores the behavioral implications of His life in our soul and body. Living, as we do, in a restless world, it is important that we understand that the true "rest" that Jesus intends for us (cf. Matt. 11:28) can only be experienced in spiritual union with Christ and allowing His life to be lived out through our behavior.

The Issue is JESUS: Daily Thoughts for Thoughtful Christians. This book is the prequel to the book in your hands. Like this book, it is comprised of 365 daily readings that cause the reader to focus on **JESUS** every day, while also rethinking other topics and themes as they relate to the One who is the central reality of our Christian faith. Religion has so often "majored in the minors," and it is important to be reminded daily that *The Issue is Jesus*, Christianity is Christ.

The Triune God in Christian Thought and Experience. Christian teaching on the Trinity has been both confusing and controversial. This is partially due to early Christian thinkers developing their thought on the basis of Greek philosophy rather than on the revelation of God in Jesus Christ. Using the theological categories of *theologia*, *oikonomia*, and *koinonia*, Jim seeks to take the reader into the practical experience of the Father, Son, and Holy Spirit.

Two Sides of Every Coin: The Dialectic Formatting of Christian Thought. Just as every coin has two sides, every topic within Christian thought also has at least two contrasting perspectives. These contrasts form both/and dialectics necessitating a balanced tension of complementarity between the two tenets. In this volume author Jim Fowler seeks to illustrate the dialectic formatting in various categories of Christian thought by utilizing one hundred and thirty dialectic charts.

Derivative Man: Man As God Intended. Taking John 15:1-8 as his primary text, Jim seeks to explicate that in like manner as the branch derives everything from the vine, the Christian is to derive everything from the life-source of the living Lord Jesus. Jesus explained to His disciples, "Apart from Me, you can do nothing." It is only as we are deriving everything from Jesus by faith, by means of our receptivity of His activity, that we can allow the Christ-life to be expressed.

A Commentary on the Epistle to the Galatians: The Gospel Versus Religion. Jim believes that "Galatianism" is pervasive and prevalent in the churches today, as religious legalists have duped Christians with the didactic declarations of "how-to" Christian religion in prescribed procedures, formulas, techniques and duties. The Church today is in dire need of the message of "grace and liberty" in Christ. Jim has three other commentaries in the Christocentric Commentary Series.

These and twenty other volumes authored by Jim Fowler are available on Amazon.com. Jim Fowler's Amazon author page can be viewed by going to: https://www.amazon.com/-/e/B00LWU9CHE.

Made in United States
Troutdale, OR
01/22/2024

17042984R00076